BLUE & GREEN

THE GREAT
1949 - 1989
DERBIES

BLUE & GREEN

RANGERS v CELTIC

A PERSONAL LOOK AT
THE GLASGOW DERBY BY

ARCHIE MACPHERSON

BBC BOOKS

To the family

Acknowledgements

This book could not have been written without the painstaking research and constant advice of Pat Woods, librarian and lover of football.

I would like to thank Rangers and Celtic football clubs for granting permission to speak to managers and players past and present who made invaluable contributions. My gratitude is extended to all those who were willing to talk freely about their experiences in Old Firm derby matches.

Picture Credits

Front cover Rod McLeod, back cover Colorsport.
All black and white pictures supplied by the *Glasgow Herald*, except the following: page 99 Allsport; pages 89 and 133 Colorsport; pages 54, 56–7, 59 and 108 the *Scottish Daily Record*; pages 8 and 20–1 the *Scottish Daily Record*/ROD; pages 2, 92 (both), 96, 102, 115 (both), 116, 124, 125, 127 and 135 Sportapics and page 124 Bob Thomas Sports Photography.

Published by BBC Books,
a division of BBC Enterprises Limited,
Woodlands, 80 Wood Lane, London W12 0TT
First published 1989

© Archie Macpherson 1989

ISBN 0 563 21480 5

Set in 11 on 13 point Photina (Monophoto)
Printed and bound in Great Britain by Butler & Tanner Ltd, Frome and London
Colour separations by Technik Ltd, Berkhamsted, Herts
Jacket printed by Belmont Press Ltd, Northampton

THE GREAT DERBIES

CONTENTS

Colour Section Captions

McCarthy and Drinkell in an aerial duel 20/5/89   Allsport (David Cannon)
Cooper evades McCarthy 20/5/89   Colorsport
Roberts is grounded while McStay flies 20/3/88   Colorsport
Roberts and McAvennie in balletic pose 20/3/88   Allsport (Russell Cheyne)
McMinn, Butcher and McCoist show their joy after the Skol Cup Final
26/10/86   Allsport (David Cannon)
Celtic all smiles after winning the cup 20/5/89   Allsport (David Cannon)
Morris scores and leads the celebrations 3/1/89   Allsport (Russell Cheyne)
Gough squeezes the ball past the Celtic defence for a last gasp equaliser
17/10/87   Bob Thomas Sports Photography
Woods tips the ball over the bar 20/5/89   Allsport (David Cannon)
Woods in action in the Skol Cup Final 26/10/86   Allsport (David Cannon)
Bonner leaps to thwart a Rangers' attack 20/5/89   Colorsport
McCoist on springs, Baillie and Morris admire 20/3/88   Colorsport
Walters in a tight spot 20/5/89   Colorsport

THE GREAT DERBIES

INTRODUCTION

Blue and green are the primary colours of Scottish football. They associate not just with Rangers and Celtic football clubs but also with a culture which is keen to perpetuate beliefs that have little to do with association football and much to do with an eccentric view of the history of Scotland and Ireland. They denote tribal loyalties and signify a lot about where your cradle was, your school, your church, your friends and your turnstiles. The colours are splashed not only throughout Scotland but appear, like the Coca-Cola sign, in the most surprising places around the world; and like the famous drink they give the global wanderer the feeling that civilisation would not be secure without their presence. Thus it is one of the enduring experiences in life to be swamped, as I have been, by expatriates wearing the colours in New York, Toronto, Melbourne, Rio or Hong Kong, enjoying their hospitality and listening to them rhyme off facts about Rangers and Celtic as if the remembrance of their Scottish footballing catechism is the very stuff that makes exile just about bearable.

It all began on 28 May 1888 when 2000 people turned up to see Rangers and Celtic play their first game against each other. Afterwards the players retired to a local hall where they shared a tea and engaged in some harmonious singing. This seems so remote from the sectarian clamour of the contemporary terraces that we might well be looking back to two teams partaking of tiffin after a chukka of polo in Simla. If that distant past takes us to what appears to be a rather foreign country, then by the turn of the century we begin to see something resembling the more familiar confrontations which were to dominate Scottish football for so long, because it was at about that time that someone dubbed the two clubs the 'Old Firm'. It is not clear who first coined the phrase, but it indicated a certain cynicism by someone who believed them to have become motivated by more than simply the love of the sport. They had in fact developed a keen commercial attitude in an age when amateurism was still extolled but, like the hansom cab, was running out of time. They knew they were good box-office, and this was even before sectarianism had raised its head to any great degree. Crowds flocked to see them. They each knew that in effectively driving that grand old club, Queen's Park, off the scene they were going to be good for one another. The Old Firm had settled down to compete for possession of the new twentieth century.

It is said that the introduction of workers from Harland and Wolff from Belfast to establish a shipyard on the Clyde around 1912 brought about the Irish and sectarian dimension which has enveloped the clubs ever since. From about that time signings of a so-called religious nature began to be made until the rivalry reached its full throttle just after the First World War and it became something of an established public perception that Rangers rigidly signed only Protestants and Celtic, more flexibly, mainly Catholics. This changed in July 1989 when Rangers signed Maurice Johnston. The Union Jack and the tricolour of the Republic of Ireland have since come to represent emblems of terrace approval of origins and upbringing which, although this may remain mystifying even to many Scots, have a real and significant pull on those who flaunt them on match days. As this book is not about churches but about football and its effect on people, it does not delve too far into the origins of any bigotry. Nor does it seek to analyse it in any depth. But as it is set in Glasgow, it is impossible to write about this famous derby without the religious aspect surfacing within the appropriate context. It would also be quite unrealistic not to preface anything about the Old Firm with reference to the social background which makes the derby game between the two quite unique.

Its history is replete with magnificent games. It has uplifted the depressed, depressed the uplifted, mortified bookies, influenced the Scottish divorce rate, survived riots, withstood a disaster, created legends, spawned a million jokes and bored hardly anybody. However questionable its underlying nature might be, its huge appeal has never been in doubt. As long ago as September 1898 a crowd of 44 868 watched the game at Celtic Park, and in 1913 there were 65 000 inside Ibrox for the traditional Ne'erday meeting, with thousands locked outside. The fixture was hardly exhausting its popularity when, on 2 January 1939, the two clubs set a record attendance for a League game in Great Britain with 118 567 at Ibrox.

This book begins with the post-war period and examines the derby games which have had a bearing of one kind or another on the development of the clubs since then. It starts as Bill Struth of Rangers was beginning to get old and a relatively unknown ex-miner called Jock Stein was playing centre-half for Albion Rovers. If Stein was unsure of what the future held for him, then so was society as a whole as it experienced the birth pains of the Welfare State. The only certain thing one can say of the period is that Rangers and Celtic supporters were uncommonly united in seeing the quality of life in general as being influenced by only two factors: victory or defeat.

"What do you mean you're a neutral?"

CHAPTER ONE

PEACE IN OUR TIME

There was never any possibility that the coming of peace in 1945 would mellow the vast throngs of Rangers and Celtic supporters who returned from the war prepared to believe in the dawning of a golden age, but equally convinced that whatever they had fought for would not refashion the historical divisions in Scotland which were to prove more durable than the Siegfried Line. They returned to the kind of football hostility that they knew and loved so well. The carnage involved in beating Adolf Hitler seemed to have had little effect on those who encouraged the belief, on Old Firm match days, that the brotherhood of man was an impossible concept. Segregation was a word better known in Glasgow than in perhaps any city outside the Deep South of the United States, as supporters benignly accepted separate entrances and terraces in a way which then astonished the outsider but which is now almost universal practice throughout the world of football. Segregation of Old Firm crowds always seemed regrettable but eminently sensible, and the war certainly did nothing to narrow the chasm between the two sides.

There were certain consolations in that period of austerity shortly after the war, and perhaps the most accessible of these was watching professional football. The game gorged itself with people, while perhaps at the same time paying scant attention to their creature comforts – thus sowing the seeds for its own partial demise in later decades. There was particular interest in Glasgow. The huge crowds that flocked after Rangers and Celtic were sustained above all by reciprocal hatred, and little was done publicly to reduce the tensions springing from religious antagonism. It was commercial after all. The Horst Wessel song having been put to flight, Rangers' supporters could come back home to rollicking choruses of 'The Sash My Father Wore' and the Celtic fans to 'Kevin Barry'. The war had not induced amnesia.

As society was being reconstructed and the Welfare State being established alongside the deprivations of rationing and power cuts, one of the few extravagances of the age was the passion and fury of the Old Firm supporters. They chased controversy like people seeking extra food coupons, for without it their lives would have been diminished. The feast they enjoyed most of all was at Ibrox Stadium on 27 August 1949 in a game between the two clubs which will be remembered above all for two names: Cox and Tully.

Charlie Tully and Sammy Cox had little in common. Cox was a beautifully balanced defender who had a tackle like a trap snapping; Tully was a dawdling, meandering ball player of genius. Cox could have marketed Brylcreem as successfully as did Johnny Haynes in a later era, while Tully wore a dishevelled look that itself seemed suited to his cavalier approach to the game. Cox belonged to and was a direct product of that age of supremacy engineered by the manager, Bill Struth; Tully was an import who represented the most formidable challenge to Rangers since the end of the war. Cox was an Ayrshire Protestant; Tully was a Belfast Catholic. From the viewpoint of the terraces, these men seemed to exemplify what the two clubs were all about.

A crowd of 95 000 turned up at Ibrox that Saturday. They had scrambled and bargained for tickets all the previous week. The natural interest in this particular game was accentuated by other factors, not the least of which was the entry of Charles Patrick Tully into the Scottish scene. He was signed from Belfast Celtic in June 1948 for £8000 and immediately lent subtlety to the side, captivating the Celtic support, whose loyalty to a club almost perpetually overshadowed by the opposition was frequently stretched to the limit. Tully rekindled their faith when only weeks after his début at Celtic Park he inspired the side to a surprising 3–1 win over their old rivals. He must have enjoyed this as much as anyone, for Belfast is not a million miles away from Glasgow and could almost be said to be a thriving suburb of the Old Firm's fief. Consequently he would have known from the cradle what victory over Rangers meant.

The war had not dented Rangers' status as Scotland's premier club. They had retained some of their key players who had not gone to fight but worked in posts in industry. But the factor which aided this continuity more than any other was the dominating personality of one of the great managers of all time, Bill Struth. His portrait still stares down from the trophy room at Ibrox with a square-jawed virility which is etched with self-assurance. Struth, though, was as remote from tactics and coaching techniques as the chairman of a multi-national is from the shop-room floor. But it was he, above all else, who was the architect of Rangers' style, conviction and arrogance.

The statistics of the immediate post-war era offer adequate explanation for Rangers' self-belief and Celtic's frustration. In the three seasons from 1946 to 1949, in twelve matches in national and domestic competition, Rangers had won nine victories to Celtic's two, with one drawn. But then in 1949, with more than a suggestion of *anno domini* creeping up on Rangers' captain, Jock 'Tiger' Shaw, Celtic in the first of the League Cup sectional games at Parkhead beat Rangers 3–2. Two weeks later they made for Ibrox for the return game, with the thought uppermost in Celtic supporters' minds that it was conceivable that the Struth era of invincibility was drawing to a close.

| 27 August 1949 | **Rangers 2 Celtic 0** | Ibrox Stadium |
| | (League Cup sectional match) | |

Rangers: Brown, Young, Shaw, Cox, Woodburn, Rae, Waddell, Findlay, Thornton, Duncanson, Rutherford

Celtic: Miller, Mallan, Baillie, Evans, Boden, McAuley, Collins, McPhail, Johnston, Tully, Haughney

Scorers: Findlay (40), Waddell (83)

Referee: A.B. Gebbie (Hamilton)   *att*: 95 000

Charlie Tully's love affair
with green and white
hoops was inevitably
interrupted by marriage

Willie Thornton of Rangers went to the stadium that day knowing that, whatever the pressure involved, his club had the bonus of a defence which had rightly earned its title, the 'Iron Curtain'.

🔊 To be honest I got fed up hearing about the Iron Curtain. All right, we had a great defence, I know that. But in fact if you look back Rangers also had one of the best forward lines in their history. We didn't score as many goals as some other eras but we scored when it mattered and that's what counts, surely? That day we got the normal brief talk from Bill Struth. As usual he advised us to kick with the wind if we won the toss and he reminded us about the bonus. He never forgot to mention the bonus. That was the extent of our team talk.'

John McPhail of Celtic in the other dressing-room was hardly in receipt of any more advice.

🔊 Jimmy McGrory, our manager, was one of nature's gentlemen and said very little to us. He was much less of an influence in the dressing-room than Bob Kelly, the chairman. Bob could be a very stern man when he liked and autocratic, but he was also a wonderful man when you were in a crisis and he had a simple belief that football should be played with two wingers and a man going through the middle. There wasn't really much discussion. And, of course, we were always reminded that we were playing for the jerseys above all else.'

So against a background of preparation that by modern standards would be considered almost dereliction of duty, both teams ran out into the bright sunshine of Ibrox. At the start, according to a contemporary report, Celtic looked 'as if they were playing in somebody's benefit match. Their inter-passing was delightful.' This was hardly an unusual pattern and seems to have been repeated countless numbers of times during that decade. But, almost habitually, Celtic's ability to entertain was far removed from their capacity to win.

On this particular day, though, Rangers' normally inflexible and routine choice of team had undergone an unusual change. Ian McColl, the erect and intelligent engineering graduate who had signally failed his preliminaries against Charlie Tully in the first match, was not playing. Rangers had moved Sammy Cox from his normal left-sided position to the right, giving rise to the belief (still maintained to this day) that this was part of a strategy of confrontation, because it was there that Cox, the uncompromising tackler, was bound to meet up with the elusive Tully. But it was not, in fact, such a ploy. Sammy Cox himself offers a more mundane reason.

> An hour before kick-off Ian McColl walked into the dressing-room wearing a big heavy coat and a muffler round his neck. Remember, this was August and the weather was marvellous. He announced he had a terrible cold and wasn't fit enough to play. He hadn't even phoned in to warn us about it. We couldn't believe it. Mr Struth took one look at me and said, "Sam, move over to right-half and get Willie Rae out of the stand in your position." Now we all knew that Willie, realising earlier he wasn't going to be playing, had something like a sixteen-course meal at the Ivy restaurant before the match, so you can imagine he was in a right good condition for it! But it had to be done. That's how I came to be playing right-half that day.'

The consensus view of the reporters present was that the game as a football match lasted only twenty minutes. Sammy Cox remembers that infamous moment when Celtic were pressing hard and the clash came.

> I went after the ball and turned, wanting to push it out of the penalty area. I knew Tully was close by me and I was certainly determined not to give him the freedom that Ian McColl had at Celtic Park. But as I kicked it I felt this sharp dig on my ankle and knew it was Charlie. I turned and kicked him. I admit that. I kicked him just above the shin-guard and said, "Don't do that to me again." It was a jab with the toe more than anything else and I was surprised to see him rolling around on the ground as if I had booted him in the family jewels. Then I knew the crowd had reacted.'

Sammy Cox's account, especially years afterwards, cannot tell the whole story and understandably, whilst an admission of sorts has been made, he would certainly not want to push the self-destruct button. It has therefore to be viewed with caution, particularly since Charlie Tully is sadly no longer alive to tell his version. Cox claims some sort of provocation, and that is something which must remain unconfirmed. But at least at one end of the ground and in the press box it was evident that Tully, for whatever reason, had clearly been kicked. It was also stated by many people present that day that Tully had grossly over-reacted.

The Celtic end witnesses close to the incident obviously saw it as an unprovoked attack on an irreproachable idol. As Tully lay writhing in the Rangers' penalty area the supporters quickly contributed to the proceedings. As one report had it, 'Bottles were merrily doing their "Pennies from Heaven" act.' Fights broke out on the terraces, in that mysterious way they had, amongst supporters of the same colours, and the section at the bottom spilled out over on to the track, thus giving the impression in that unstable atmosphere that the pitch was about to be invaded. Jack McGinn, who was later to become chairman of Celtic, was in the crowd as a young teenager and ran to the top of the terrace; he recalls an old man saying, 'If you run they'll think you threw the bottles. Take it easy.' He remembers: 'The sky was black with flying glass. We just had to duck and hope for the best.' John McPhail was standing some distance away beside his marker Willie Woodburn, the Rangers' centre-half. 'I said to Ben [Woodburn's nick-name], "In the name of God! If they get on the park I bet I can beat you to the dressing-room."'

The police waded in as only they could. Within minutes the youngsters at the front of the crowd had been shepherded back to the terraces, arrests had been made, the bottle throwers from the top of the terraces had disappeared and the casualties had been escorted away. Play was stopped for about four minutes while order was restored; to some it had seemed like an eternity.

Bobby Collins, the diminutive Celtic winger, didn't feel much panic himself.

> Honestly, I was so engrossed in the game that it didn't really bother me all that much. I recall us standing around wondering what was going to happen and chatting to Rangers players, but then we got under way again. And knowing Charlie I doubt if he was totally blameless. I remember he could easily drive you up the wall. He once caused me to lose my temper on the golf course when he deliberately made me miss a putt in a needle game when he distracted me on the final green. I almost went for him with my putter; then I burst out laughing. I just don't think Cox would have kicked him for nothing.'

John McPhail well realised that Charlie was aware of his audience.

> In a previous game at Celtic Park Charlie was tackled by Woodburn and rolled over and over as if he was dying. Woodburn went for him and I remember thinking, Charlie's not going to live through this, for Ben had a terrible temper when he got going. But all he did was rush over and stop short and shout at Charlie, "I suppose you're doing this for something to write about in your column on Monday," referring to Charlie's newspaper articles. Charlie started to laugh and when I saw Ben smiling I knew Charlie was safe.'

Tully and Cox picked themselves up and got on with the game in front of an astonished assembly who could not believe that the referee, A. B. Gebbie, had taken no action of any sort. But John McPhail believes that at least the players on the day recovered quickly, although they had naturally been affected to some degree.

> Really it was all over in a flash. The crowd certainly kept it going on. But we just got on with the game. There might have been some more dig in the tackles but honestly nobody really went out of control – but as you know, if you're getting a lot of aggro from the terraces it can sometimes look worse than it is. I think what did happen, though, is that we lost our rhythm. No doubt about that, and certainly not surprisingly Charlie became less effective. I began to get the old feelings in the bones again that the tide was going to run against us.'

It did. Rangers, as they so often had in that era, used their direct strength to score twice. Willie Findlay netted after Waddell had hammered a shot against goalkeeper Willie Miller five minutes from half-time, and Waddell himself scored the second seven minutes from the end after a solo run through the middle. In between, George Young actually missed a penalty. But these statistics were overshadowed by the Cox–Tully incident and it was that which preoccupied people for such a long time afterwards, rather than the result itself.

It seemed astonishing then – and still does now – that Cox was not sent off for a foul which was clearly seen by everybody – although apparently not by the referee, who was closer than most. This fact merely fuelled the abiding belief of Celtic Football Club that referees were more kindly disposed towards

A football manager who became a tsar. Bill Struth whose commandments dominated a generation

the other side than to them, and the feeling was compounded by the ultimate decision of the examining Scottish Football Association (SFA) disciplinary committee who merely reprimanded both players and admitted that the referee had erred in taking no action. This did not settle the affair. As a small boy I remember cowering in terror watching a fight on a bus in Glasgow between two men who were ultimately separated by an angel of mercy dressed as a housewife wielding a shopping-bag in her hand like a mallet. They had been fighting about Cox and Tully. The clash of the two players had touched on primitive instincts and unleashed aggravations that were to linger on for years.

The incident had seemed to confirm the theory that what was demonstrated on the terraces was mirrored by players on the field of play; that there was a sub-stratum of religious street politics to this game. When players from that era are asked about this they are quite adamant that no such feelings existed on the park. And yet this contradiction contains for me a certain coyness, as if outwardly they had to exhibit an almost unattainable purity but that deeper feelings did exist. Indeed, if they had not then the game would not have been elevated to its unique level of commitment. Perhaps what we can deduce is that most players under the circumstances shielded themselves from the more malicious sentiments of the terraces and allowed football to sublimate any particular feelings they may have had towards the opposition.

Sammy Cox:

> 'I never said anything of a religious nature to Charlie Tully. I know the story got around that I did, but I deny it. I never did to anyone during these games. I played hard, and why shouldn't I have? The Celtic players did as well.'

John McPhail:

> 'Never at any time in my entire career did I hear a single religious remark made to me by any Rangers' player. Sure, we were desperate to win. But it stayed at that.'

Bobby Collins:

> 'Religion? Nobody gave it a thought. I know it was in the background and that you made special efforts during these games to please your own supporters, but we just got on with it. If we really had been like some of our supporters it would have been mayhem every game and, of course, it was nothing of the kind.'

Celtic continued with their protest to the Scottish Football Association, but despite all their pleas could not gain a transcript of the proceedings which took place in the SFA committee. They felt sinned against, and Tully later found himself in further trouble with the SFA for apparently trying to lead players from the field in another Old Firm game, headed, in the eyes of the aggrieved Celtic supporters, towards martyrdom. And to the public it was all confirmation that the shared mistrust of the supporters was rigid and absolute. Indeed, it remains to this day quite noteworthy that many loyal supporters of both clubs will shun this fixture either because they cannot stand the atmosphere or feel the tension to be unbearable.

The day after the incident, however, as Sammy Cox relates, there was no sense of recrimination.

> Charlie came down to Kilmarnock to see me on the Sunday. The newspaper he wrote for contacted me and asked if it was all right if they came to take a picture. Charlie, who was a delightful bloke, sat with me and the family as if we had just had a party the day before. You wouldn't have thought we had caused a rude word, let alone a near riot. He told me afterwards that Bob Kelly had been incensed that he'd gone anywhere near me. But Charlie was a law unto himself. That's what made him such an entertainer.'

It made an odd tableau. There were the two players in a posed and artificial setting of innocuous domesticity, pandering to the notion that by being seen together like that they would soothe the savage breast of Glasgow. One doubts if the Second Coming would have done that! But at least it could be said that Cox and Tully had taken many minds off the privations of austerity in the country, encouraging its population to believe that the most central feature of their lives was an Old Firm match. This has proved even yet to be the most durable form of Glaswegian escapism.

Willie Waddell. A product of the Struth dynasty

CHAPTER TWO

A WORLD APART

At about 3.30 p.m.* on the afternoon of 19 October 1957 a certain BBC technician in London left his particular job in the recording room to get himself a cup of tea. He had only about ten minutes to get from his post to the canteen and back again, because the duration of his tea break was identical with the half-time interval at a football match being played some 500 miles away in front of 82 293 people. He made sure he completed the trip in time, because his role that day was to record the game which was being sent electronically down a line from Hampden Park, Glasgow to the recording machines in London.

Comparing contemporary methods with the system then would be like contrasting the lap-top computer with the abacus. Today the transmission is automatic, immediate and with instant replay; then it was laborious and comparatively primitive. A camera had to be set up in front of a television screen and, quite simply, a film was taken of the pictures on the monitor. The film was later edited and transmitted. But it wasn't that night, because something went terribly wrong.

When the technician had gone off for his break he had, like anybody meticulous about his trade, turned off the camera and clipped a cover over the lens for dust protection. When he returned he switched on the camera in plenty of time, but forgot the lens cap. It stayed on. So it was that the entire second half of one of the most famous games in Scottish footballing history was lost to posterity. Gone from public television record were six goals, crowd trouble, mounted police on the terraces, a bottle barrage on the running track and the raising of the Cup which, for Celtic supporters that afternoon, might have signified the coming of a new millennium.

It was a hard one to explain away to the exultant supporters. One of the stories which seemed to gain credibility, although quite untrue, was that the film had been destroyed on the direct instructions of the then BBC sports editor in Scotland, Peter Thomson, who throughout his career was dubbed 'Blue Peter' and who that evening had to go on screen to explain to the public that the second half had vanished. He must have felt like a bank manager telling a client that his life savings had just been pilfered. This notion of editorial involvement in some form of censoring was given credence by Celtic Football Club itself, whose members never really believed the explanation offered and felt there was something sinister afoot – given their long-held belief that the media in Scotland were in any case nothing more than a large-scale public relations arm of Rangers Football Club. Even years later, when Celtic had run

* This particular derby kicked off at 2.45 p.m. to allow enough light for any extra-time.

In Celtic's blitzkrieg Neil Mochan stayed modestly out of picture on this occasion. His shot, however, did not stay out of the net for Celtic's fifth goal

up a significant victory and I was there with the cameras, Jock Stein would smile wickedly at me, as only he knew how, and say, 'Did you get the dust cover off the camera this time?'

Football was running scared of television. By that time almost 800 British cinemas had closed in the space of six years as people on the wave of full employment, and buoyed up by the dubious morality of Harold Macmillan's 'You've never had it so good', went out and bought TVs in their millions. One suspected that the age of the twentieth-century troglodyte had begun and, indeed, suspicion of the new mass medium spawned resentment and bred fear. In a city which saw one major newspaper, the *Evening News*, fold that very year of 1957 because of a slump in sales, a sister paper, *The Bulletin*, wrote in apprehension of the nation's apparent moral decline as seen through falling attendances in the Church of Scotland, indicating that television had the ability to 'satisfy the demands of the majority, supplementing the Sunday newspapers' diet of crime, sex and sensation'.

As one probably recalls Muffin the Mule more vividly than anything else of that era, one might detect an over-reaction in these words. But that same feeling could well have been discerned in the views of the then chairman of Celtic Football Club, Robert Kelly. He viewed televised football with outright distaste and rightly saw that it could threaten attendances at football matches. In that year of 1957 Celtic toured America and Kelly saw at first hand what television, admittedly in a more advanced state, was doing to baseball and boxing attendances. As one of the game's acknowledged visionaries, he began to hand out warnings. He was eventually to move to the more extreme view of advocating that anyone who even appeared on the box for any reason ought to be banned from football for a year. His more moderate proposal for live coverage of a match was that television could do it but only if they would cough up sixpence a head for everyone who watched it in their homes.

However, despite his aversion to the medium he, too, must have been disappointed that later that evening he could not settle down at the regular time of ten o'clock to relive this triumph.

---

19 October 1957   **Celtic 7   Rangers 1**   Hampden Park
(League Cup Final)

Celtic: Beattie, Donnelly, Fallon, Fernie, Evans. Peacock, Tully, Collins, McPhail, Wilson, Mochan

Rangers: Niven, Shearer, Caldow, McColl, Valentine, Davis, Scott, Simpson, Murray, Baird, Hubbard

Scorers: Wilson (23), Mochan (45,75), McPhail (53,68,80), Fernie (90, pen.); Simpson (56))

Referee: J.A. Mowat (Burnside)   *att*: 82 293

Rangers had lost a centre-half. The great George Young, a sentinel not just for a team on the park but of the Struth tradition of success through solid defence, had retired the previous summer. The continuity of Rangers' strength in that position had been broken by the suspension *sine die* of Willie Woodburn. They had tried out wing-half Ian McColl, now beginning to be regarded as a veteran, and a reserve wing-half, Willie Moles, who was actually suffering from eye trouble. There being no immediate answer to their problem they turned to a man playing for Queen's Park – one John Valentine, a large and hearty player who hailed from Blairgowrie and who was eventually given the awesome task of trying to make the Rangers supporters forget Woodburn and Young. It was a mistake of epic proportion. Rangers' Bobby Shearer, not notably given to nerves, felt uneasy before the game.

'I can't be anything other than honest and say I was terrified about what might happen to us right through the middle. Now that might sound like being clever and trying to dodge my own responsibilities that day. But the fact is that although Big John was a nice big guy he really should never have been at Ibrox. He just wasn't up to it. In fact, to this day I am convinced that Scot Symon signed Valentine because he was pressurised by the press into it, and also because he had heard Celtic were interested in him. It doesn't matter whether they were or not. Just the fact that he had heard about a sniff of Celtic interest was enough to bring him to Ibrox. I could tell right away in the early part of the game that he was going to have a nightmare against Billy McPhail. That made us nervous and to be honest it began to spread right through the team.'

Celtic had been given a considerable boost that season in having a month earlier recorded their first win at Ibrox in a League game since the war. They had needed it, for since 1949 and the Cox–Tully incident they had signally failed to replace Rangers as the dominant Scottish club, even though under the captaincy of Jock Stein they had followed up their winning of the Scottish Cup in 1951 by achieving the League and Scottish Cup double in 1954. Since the end of the 1940s Rangers had won four League titles and two Scottish Cups and had, unlike Celtic, participated in European competition. Billy

McPhail recalls that, despite the earlier win that season, Rangers went into the Final as clear favourites.

6   We thought this was unrealistic but it was a kind of familiar situation for us to be in against Rangers, and to be honest I cannot remember there was any undue anxiety or tension as we got ready for the match. I suddenly remembered as I walked out on to the park the words that old Paddy Travers had said to me when I first joined Clyde: "Keep the head, quick bursts and shoot." I actually scored a goal in ten seconds when I made my début for the Clyde, so starting off well was always important to me in a game. Now we didn't score all that quickly but I just thought it was our day when Charlie Tully fastened on to a quick shy and the ball went from him against the far post, then right along the goal-line, hit the other one and then was cleared. From then on I didn't think their luck could last.'

Jack Mowat was the referee whom the Glasgow police had asked the Scottish Football Association to appoint for every Rangers and Celtic game to be played, because of the respect he commanded both in his own country and abroad. Indeed, he was to go on later to referee one of the greatest games of all time, Real Madrid against Eintracht in the European Cup Final at Hampden Park in 1960. Between 1953, when he refereed the first Scottish Cup game between Rangers and Celtic in twenty-five years, and 1960 he officiated at virtually every Old Firm game. His authority was unassailable. He had the virtue of appearing to merge into the background and only materialise when required, along with a sharp sense of due reprimand and unflamboyant control. He recalls:

6   It was a typical edgy, nervy start. In that sense you expect some fouls, and we got them early on. I warned three Rangers and one Celtic player although I only booked one, Sammy Baird. I remember that John Valentine looked decidedly ill at ease from the start and his clumsiness was apparent. I certainly was going to make sure that if anybody was going to try to play football they would get protection from me.'

Mowat was praised unanimously by the press for having allowed the game to flow. And since it did, the wide acres of Hampden stimulated one man in particular to a performance of grandeur, and from the mainstream of his play the entire Celtic side became an irresistible tidal wave. His name was Willie Fernie. Billy McPhail, who was to score a hat-trick, modestly relegates himself to a position of some insignificance when he talks about his colleague.

6   Willie Fernie did the carving up. It was one of those games when you could say he reached perfection. Sometimes Willie tried too much and you would go away thinking he was a greedy player who couldn't part with the ball when he should. And certainly that was his biggest flaw. That day I can well remember that the ball seemed tied to his boot and they just couldn't stop him. He had that beautiful upright running action that gave the impression he was sitting almost back in his heels when he moved with the ball a stride ahead. He had a great build with the strongest-looking pair of thighs I've ever seen on a player. Early on in the game he went on a run and swept past the entire Rangers defence and crossed. I got my head to the ball and it came off the cross-bar with the Rangers goalkeeper well beaten. You just felt, even though we missed, that he was going to dictate to the rest of us.'

Modesty has always been one of Billy's principal virtues, but we musn't allow it to distort the picture of that day, for in truth without his clear-cut superiority in the air over Valentine and his quickness of foot round the box, all that Fernie began to lay on might have been much less fruitful. McPhail had formed a partnership in the forward line with Sammy Wilson which on the face of it had seemed highly unlikely. Wilson was a free transfer from St Mirren and McPhail, who ought to have been transferred to Celtic much earlier than he actually was, could hardly be said to have been in the first flush of youth. Yet they dovetailed at times as if they had formed their partnership in the cradle.

Their first goal might well have been considered a matter of their stage routine: a high ball to McPhail, a header from him to the feet of the advancing Wilson and the ball sent to the net from his foot. It had happened before in other League games, but when it happens in a Cup Final against Rangers at Hampden the old routine does tend to take on a new glow. They had established their bridgehead.

> ' We had the wind at our backs and the ball was running for us. The pitch, which was supposed to be heavy after all the rain and supposed to suit Rangers more, didn't prove any kind of handicap to us. Now to be honest, even one up and going strong you never feel all that relaxed in an Old Firm game. If a team comes back at you in these games and scores a goal it's a huge uplift for them. But what really turned the scales was the goal just before half time by Neil Mochan. I recall him going along the line after leaving two defenders behind him and he hit this shot from an amazing angle. Maybe if he had tried it a hundred times it might not have come off for him, but it almost took the net away. I think that was the turning point.'

Hints of disintegration were in the air for Rangers. Valentine was struggling, Shearer could do nothing against the thrusts of Mochan, and Willie Fernie seemed to be moving at will through the Rangers defence. Then, with that dust cap still firmly in its place on the lens in London, Celtic vaulted into command led by Billy McPhail, who was to achieve something that few players in his club could manage: a hat-trick against their oldest enemy.

> ' To be honest it's a bit of a blur now because it was a blur then. We were doing so well; I suppose I wasn't taking it all in. I just recall Willie Fernie weaving his way down the touchline and then swinging it high over for me and me getting up as high as I could and my head getting beyond Valentine's and the ball ending up in the net. I suppose that sounds simple, but that's how I recall it. But the second one I remember best of all because I recall a photograph later of me standing up in front of the Rangers goal with about five of their players lying on the ground after I had taken a ball that had come back off the cross-bar from my own shot and hitting the rebound past Niven.'

Even a goal for Rangers by Billy Simpson, the Ulsterman, lobbing the ball past Beattie to make the score 3–1 eleven minutes into the second half could not stem the increasing disarray of the Rangers defence, which now fell apart. Then came an astonishing sequence of scoring at a rate far in excess of the average Old Firm game. McPhail scored his second goal described above, seven minutes later Mochan scored with a vicious left-foot shot after a cross from Wilson had eluded the entire Rangers defence, and to make it six McPhail

By the time Willie Fernie had scored Celtic's seventh, George Niven had developed a crick in his neck

himself scored a goal which was later described as one of the best of that year when he jumped to head the ball past Valentine, swept round him, controlled it and then ran on to slide it past Niven. In the final minute McPhail was brought down and Celtic were awarded a penalty kick.

> Charlie Tully came up to me and said, 'Take it, Billy. Nobody's ever scored four goals against the Rangers. Go on, take it.' I didn't take long to make up my mind. Three was enough for me. One hat-trick against Rangers in the Cup Final was about as good as you could get. And supposing I had missed it. It would maybe have taken a little bit of the gloss off it. I said "No thanks".'

It was then the crowd started to spill over on to the running track as fights broke out at the Rangers end of the ground and bottles, in a depressingly familiar manner, rained down on those at the front. Jack Mowat, the referee, watched on in concern.

> I saw the crowd coming over and for a moment I got very worried, but really, although it looked bad at the time, I knew the police would control it quickly and they did. I was more concerned about getting the game under way as soon as possible. So after just about a couple of minutes of stoppage I ordered the penalty to be taken, which Willie Fernie of Celtic took and scored. I

remember days afterwards meeting Willie Allison, a famous Scottish journalist who, of course, was supposed to be neutral in these things. I met him walking towards me down Buchanan Street and when he completely ignored me I shouted after him. He turned to me and said, "What were you doing awarding a penalty to Celtic in the last minute?" "Because it was a penalty," I answered. "But giving them a penalty. How could you?" I suppose that says it all.'

Billy McPhail then experienced that well-known corollary of euphoria: a sense of anti-climax.

There we were with the Cup after the most famous victory in the history of the club and I just couldn't take it all in. We celebrated all right, but it was as if we had just gone out and done a day's work and come back home for our tea. I don't think it was until days after that it truly sank in what we had achieved that day.'

Bobby Shearer tried to hide.

We went back to the St Enoch hotel. I couldn't look anybody in the face. I wanted to disappear, but it wasn't easy. In fact, I had to travel back to Hamilton with the wife in a train and I remember I had to restrain myself at what a Rangers supporter was shouting at me. When we got back home I sat down on the couch we had bought for the house we had just moved into. Three years later, when we got the couch re-upholstered, my wife found something that had slipped down the inside of the cover. It was my runners-up medal that I hadn't seen since that night. Frankly, I thought I had thrown it away. It was like something coming back to haunt me.'

The Celtic supporters were reluctant to leave Hampden Park, but when they did it was to be as creators of new art forms. From the parodying of the current Harry Belafonte ditty 'Oh Island in the Sun' to 'Celtic Seven and Rangers One', to epic poems, emotional sonnets, banners and graffiti incorporating the famous score in a manner that any pop artist would have been proud of, they were establishing such a variety of memory aids that the ultimate triumph of the day must now be seen as the supporters making the error of that television technician in London a total irrelevance.

CHAPTER THREE

THE GREAT SHOW STOPPER

If Philip Larkin had ever met Jim Baxter he might well have seen in him something which reflected the era which so fascinated the English poet. Larkin wrote about the 'Swinging Sixties', whilst Baxter played his football. Larkin recognised that the age of permissiveness began in 1963 at the time of the Profumo affair, which brought down a prime minister. Baxter was forcing us to rewrite our definitions of elegance and arrogance as he frequently introduced even talented opposition to the dubious pleasures of footballing bondage.

Larkin wrote:

> Sexual intercourse began
> In nineteen sixty-three
> (Which was rather late for me)
> Between the end of the Chatterley ban
> And the Beatles' first LP.

Baxter tattooed his name over a city with deeds of style on the park and legends of socialising off it. The age seemed as right for him as it appeared inappropriate to a middle-aged poet whose regret for the passing of his youth would only have been heightened if week after week he had been able to watch the slim figure in blue dictating the agenda of the game with an apparent ease which suggested he would be the only player afield who wouldn't need an anti-perspirant afterwards. The 'Swinging Sixties' had a footballer who did not need much encouragement to catch the mood of the times and who was releasing his club, Rangers, from the conventions of orthodox thinking through an imagination which was both highly fertile and shocking. You do not sit on a ball during a football match, nor do you stuff the ball up your jersey as you are about to be presented with the cup. Baxter did both, of course. It delighted, enraged and shocked all at once, just as other things, from Carnaby St to the Liverpool 'Cavern', were also doing. If our thinking was still rather prudish in Scotland by comparison with the South, Baxter on a football park might have been indicating that the days of the strait-lace were numbered.

He may have given better performances than that of the evening of 15 May 1963 at Hampden Park in a replay of the Final of the Scottish Cup against Celtic, but it was on that occasion that all the elements of his personality seemed to fit perfectly together.

The teams had drawn 1–1 on a wet and windy Saturday on 4 May. Rangers

15 May 1963	**Rangers 3 Celtic 0**	Hampden Park
	(Scottish Cup Final replay)	

Rangers: Ritchie, Shearer, Provan, Greig, McKinnon, Baxter, Henderson, McMillan, Millar, Brand, Wilson

Celtic: Haffey, Mackay, Kennedy, McNamee, McNeill, Price, Craig, Murdoch, Divers, Chalmers, Hughes.

Scorers: Brand (7,71), Wilson (44)

Referee: T. Wharton (Clarkston)   *att*: 120 273

had been expected to win, but a combination of the brilliance of the Celtic goalkeeper Haffey and the squandering of chances took the match to a replay. Ralph Brand had scored by flicking in a Henderson cross five minutes before the interval and just on the half-time whistle Bobby Murdoch equalised for Celtic. The crowd of 129 527 went home wet and bewildered. The Rangers supporters were puzzled by how their side had let Celtic off the hook, and the Celtic fans perplexed as to what side would be picked for the replay at a time when indecision seemed to be rife at Parkhead.

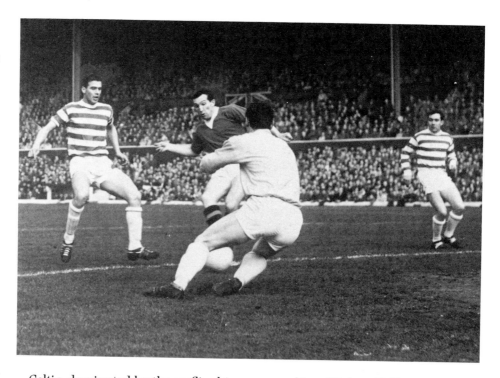

Ralph Brand, poacher supreme. Netting Rangers' first goal he made the keeper turn up late

Celtic, dominated by the unflinching personality of Robert Kelly, must have been aware of the deep sense of frustration that existed among their supporters because of the club's inability to solidify its position in Scottish football in the aftermath of their 7–1 drubbing of Rangers. Rather than reaching bedrock they had apparently left Hampden that day and based themselves on quicksands, for compared with their great rivals the club seemed to sink without trace over the next seven years. From that October day in 1957 until April 1965, Celtic went without a major trophy win, while Rangers picked up four League titles, four League Cups and four Scottish Cups. Players had gone from Celtic Park who might have stayed had not the chairman been determined that no one would hold the club to ransom. So Willie Fernie and Bobby Collins, seeking to improve their lot, went south. On top of that Billy McPhail and Sean Fallon had retired. The club drifted and team selections became as intriguing as the games themselves. Bobby Murdoch, as an eighteen-year-old, had played in his first Cup Final in the first match on 4 May.

To be honest I think the team selection for the replay was a disgrace. We played well on the Saturday. I know we were one down but when we fought back and played as well as Rangers after that and had our chances to win the game there was never any doubt that the same eleven would be fielded in the replay. I was quite happy with myself because I had scored the equaliser just before half-time when Bobby Shearer blocked a shot from 'Yogi' Hughes but then fell back into the net and all I had to do was slip it over the line. But I felt great and when I walked off the park I think I knew that I'd be picked again, if just for that. But then I'd heard all about the unusual selections of the teams about that period, like the time the bus was passing through Coatbridge and they saw Willie Goldie standing at the bus stop wearing a Celtic supporter's scarf, waiting to go to the game at Airdrie. They stopped to give him a lift but before the bus had stopped at the ground he was selected to play in goal. I don't know if that's strictly true, but you could almost believe it after hearing that the management had decided to change the side for the replay, dropping Jimmy Johnstone and Frank Brogan. Now I was a young lad but I know the senior players could hardly believe that they had brought in Bobby Craig, for example. I just felt then that we'd missed our chance.'

Davy Wilson, thatched with blonde hair and who formed the left side of the best Rangers forward line I have ever seen, of Henderson, McMillan, Millar, Brand and Wilson, is adamant in thinking that during that era Rangers never thought of defeat when they played Celtic.

> I admit that Celtic played better in that first game than we had anticipated, but you've also got to remember that Frank Haffey had a miraculous game for them in goal, and right at the end with the score 1–1 I missed a sitter. I remember going off the park thinking that we wouldn't let them off the hook again. The boss Scot Symon wasn't too happy with us, I can tell you. He was a remarkable man. He got very uptight about everything. I recall him at half-time in one game trying to drink a cup of tea but it was spilling all over the place because his hands were shaking with tension. And that was Stirling Albion we were playing. So you can imagine what it was like against Celtic. He didn't say much to us before the replay. He never did. It was just a case of something like, "Well, you know what to do. You wouldn't be where you are if I didn't think you could do the job. Go out and do it."'

If this was hardly the Gettysburg address, there was little danger of it being exceeded in passion in the Celtic dressing room where Bobby Murdoch, still coming to terms with life in this his first season with Celtic, was also trying to grasp the meaning behind the club's switch of personnel.

> It wasn't easy for me because I still felt kind of privileged to be playing at all, but there's no doubt that I was looking for some kind of basic instruction before the match; but it never came. I know generally speaking we were scared of Baxter and that we had been told previously to try to force him to his right side, which by comparison was almost non-existent. But all he would do was to use the outside of his left foot to combat that and we could never really pin him down in a game as a result. So we didn't even talk about that. We were resigned to the fact that Baxter was a brilliant player and we'd just have to put up with him. One very important factor was the weather. In the first game it had been wet and windy but that evening it was a perfect spring night. It was sunny and dry and I knew the ball was going to run fast, and with the kind of forward line they had I suspected the going would really suit them.'

The evening suited the crowd of 120 273. The police instruction to ban displays of provocative flags and banners went, as usual, largely unheeded and Hampden, particularly at the congested Rangers end, seemed a seamless blanket splattered with the confetti of tribal loyalty. Those supporters who had decided to stay at home and listen to events by radio were to be disappointed. Instead of the game they heard a piano recital by John Ogdon because the BBC application for a transmission had not been made in time, much to the disgust of those who preferred the male-voice choirs of the Mount Florida or King's Park ends to Tchaikovsky.

It took Rangers just seven minutes to win the Cup. While Celtic had proved in the first game that they were very often at their most resilient in adversity, Bobby Murdoch, inexperienced though he might have been, felt the tremors of collapse imminent.

> It was the very first priority, without any instruction needed, to try to avoid losing an early goal. But that's exactly what happened. Firstly they were opening us up easily. Willie Henderson was getting great service from Ian McMillan who hadn't played in the first match. He was sliding passes to him inside of Jim Kennedy and the crosses kept coming over. Then on the other side you had the direct speed of Davy Wilson. He and Ralphie Brand were similar sort of players in the way they could get off their mark quickly. They had us going back right from the start. I have to admit it now, I felt it was all up when Brand scored early on. I just couldn't see us getting back.'

Neither could the Rangers captain, Bobby Shearer, who points to a man who might well have been overshadowed by the virtuoso capabilities of Baxter but who lent considerable muscle and depth of thought to how the side performed.

> Jimmy Millar was invaluable to us. He was a real favourite of the manager's who had bought him from Dunfermline as a right-half. And I can remember well the occasion we went to Denmark on a pre-season tour. We were playing a team we should have hammered but by half-time we were struggling, I think principally because the lads had had a good night out on the town the previous night. Scot Symon came in at the interval, looked Maxie Murray straight in the eye and said, "That's the worst performance I've ever seen by a Rangers centre-forward. Jimmy Millar, you're moving up front. Put on the number nine jersey." He did and went out in the second half and scored four goals. He never looked back. I've never been sure whether Symon had been thinking of that all along or whether it was just on the spur of the moment. In any case it was one of the best moves he ever made, because Jimmy's strength and the way he could read the game helped a lot of the players around him. That night he hardly lost a ball in the tackle as I recall, and he kept dragging Billy McNeill, who had a great game in the first match, out of position to leave gaps there. And when you looked up you could always find Millar with the ball. With all that kind of running going up front, Baxter just behind in midfield was in his element.'

The lopsided genius whose left foot amply remedied any deficiencies he suffered in physique, in the tackle or in the air, and who was to design the final ignominy of the evening, had no direct hand in the first goal by Ralph Brand, which was a typical swooping effort, side-footing a cross from Henderson from six yards past Haffey who, although of occasional brilliance, would never be noted by Celtic historians as entirely predictable. But Baxter was nevertheless sliding passes of meticulous aggravation through the Celtic defence, which was not helped by the fact that they did not seem to have any cohesive form of retaliation and that the change of Jimmy Johnstone to Craig on the right was foundering simply because Craig was so sadly lacking in the pace which Johnstone certainly had. As the Rangers defence strolled with comparative ease through that first half, Baxter dictated the rhythm of the game.

Davy Wilson felt that while they were never in danger, the second goal killed all the tension.

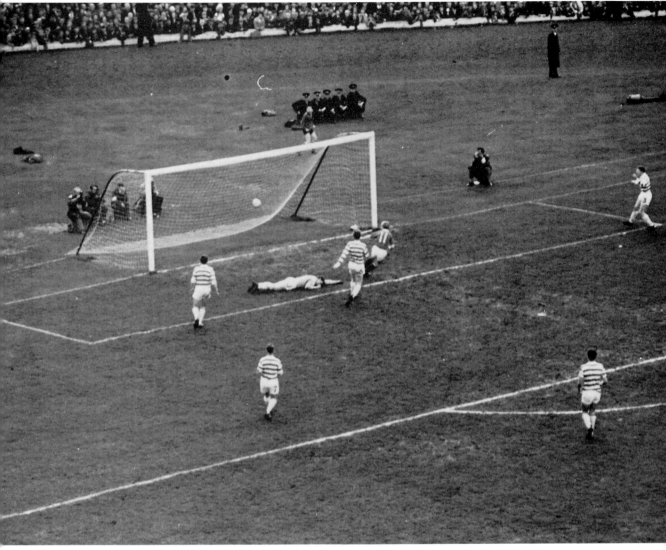

Even outnumbered in the penalty area Davy Wilson picks his spot for the second goal

> **6** I remember it was just before half-time. Now when you're so much on top and you haven't had the goals to match there's always that little nagging doubt that you could slip up. After all, Celtic came back at us in the first match. I'm not saying I was getting worried but as I watched Ralphie Brand moving in to have a shot I followed in without thinking and, lo and behold, Haffey fumbled the save and I just pounced in and stuck it away and felt this great sense of relief.'

It was now the perfect stage for Baxter to convert superiority into something approaching ridicule. Nobody could so easily suggest a feeling of contempt for less talented opponents, and while this might not have been of a conscious nature it nevertheless suited his own style of play and most certainly the hunger of his supporters who, in memory of the 7–1 defeat, would not have been averse to seeing the other half of Hampden subjected to the most severe humiliation. But it must remain a mystery why, with the ability to rub in their command of the game by reaching goal, Rangers did not press home that advantage and revenge their 7–1 defeat. Indeed, a curious lack of self-assurance emerges from Bobby Shearer, which led to an ending for which the game is most notably remembered – except by those who have deliberately expunged it from their minds.

> We were so far in front it wasn't true. Then Ralph Brand scored a funny sort of goal. He hit the ball from well outside the penalty area and it seemed to bounce in front of Haffey who was now having a nightmare. He let it slip through him and we were three up. I remember running over to the dug-out and asking how long there was to go. They told me about twenty minutes and just to keep possession as much as possible. Now if we had scored another goal right away after that and made it four, I think we might have gone for the jugular, but looking back all we wanted to do was make sure we didn't do anything stupid, so I shouted to the players just to keep the ball and not give it away. They certainly entered into the spirit of it. I'd push it to the goalkeeper who would roll it out to me, then he would throw it to our centre-half Ronnie McKinnon who would pass it back to the goalkeeper again, and so on. And then we'd give it to Baxter.'

Relieved of any further responsibilities to go forward on the instructions of his captain, and although the Rangers supporters were willing their side on to the utter destruction of the opposition, Baxter shunted the game into a lay-by of self-indulgence. He would take the ball to the touchline and juggle with it. He would put his foot on it and stand inviting the tackle like a man in a public park cavorting with a puppy. And then he simply sat on it. Baxter enthroned on a ball during a Cup Final is an enduring memory even to those, like Bobby Murdoch, who were outraged at the time.

> We were angry, to say the least. Me especially, because at that stage of the game they had put me up front and all I was doing was running around chasing shadows getting nowhere as they kept passing the ball amongst themselves without any intention of coming near our goal again. Then I saw him sit down on the ball. He's probably the only player who would get away with that. Yes, I was fuming at the way we were being treated, and yet at the same time you had to admit that you had been on the same field as one of the great players and maybe you could make an exception of him. It was in character, let's just put it that way. He had the cheek for anything.'

Not everyone in the Rangers camp condoned this unusual way of torturing the Celtic players. When they came off the field with the Cup the manager Scot Symon was waiting for them. Bobby Shearer led the way back in.

> I expected at least a hug. All I got was the manager coming straight at me, his eyes blazing: "What right had you to humiliate these Celtic players? That was outrageous." At first I thought he was kidding, but he wasn't. "You'll never do that again, believe you me." He didn't say anything directly to Jim Baxter because, to be honest, the manager treated him differently from the rest. He had to get at him through me. If you had his sort of talent I suppose you became a law unto yourself.'

It would have been harder to get a camel through the eye of a needle than to get Jim Baxter into the kingdom of ordinary men. He led an exceptional life, in possession of an exceptional talent. It burned him out. Twenty-six years later he played a bit part in a BBC television drama, 'The Gift', about a Glasgow football team. In his heyday one suspects he could have played Hamlet.

CHAPTER FOUR

THE NEW LOOK

Around the beginning of the 1960s the track-suit, that most basic of all sporting wear, became in fact something of a symbol for progress in football. Until then it had been merely a garment which provided warmth or decoration for players and only in colour did it have any distinction. But then a new breed of man began to emerge in Scottish football, and for want of a better definition he was called the 'track-suit manager'. Great play was made of this, as if we were observing the emergence of *Homo sapiens* Mark II. In truth it was something of a revolution because Scottish football had evolved slowly and gently through the years, with managerial skills being typified by such men as Bill Struth and Jimmy McGrory, who were to the actual training and coaching of players what a civil servant in the Department of Trade and Industry might be to a hod carrier on a building site.

Then on to the scene strode Jock Stein. Compared with the remoteness of daily preparation which had gone before, his involvement as manager made him seem shop-steward, master of works and a little bit of Socrates all rolled into one. His every action affirmed his belief that a manager had to sweat to attain success. To see him return from a training session in his favourite black track-suit, even in the latter stages of his career at Celtic Park, his hair dishevelled, slightly dragging his left leg and muddied from the training ground, was to see a man in a permanent state of affection for his sport.

Stein had returned to a club suffering a severe identity crisis. They were not the Celtic they had promised to be eight years earlier when they had inflicted the most injurious defeat on their famous rivals. In winning nothing else in that period it was as if Celtic had decided on an act of penance for having humiliated Rangers by giving up high drama for pantomime. They had become so indecisive and disoriented that the act of inviting Jock Stein to return seemed outrageously logical. One man made this possible, Bob Kelly, later to be knighted for his services to football. It would be erroneous to see him as simply the chairman of the club. He was also spokesman for a community. He championed Celtic causes when strong prejudicial tides occasionally turned against them and might have swamped them had his stern advocacy not been readily available and in full measure. He spoke as the leader of a minority might when representing a constituency which occasionally felt itself hard done by. Even if some of the grievances could have been illusory, and despite receiving some sore criticism from within his own ranks by those who worried about Celtic in decline on the field, he aroused mostly respect by his mix of blunt obduracy and lucid dignity which distinguished him from a surrounding sea of waffle. In many ways this worked. It gave Celtic definition. It helped

THE GREAT
1949 - 1989
DERBIES
RANGERS v CELTIC

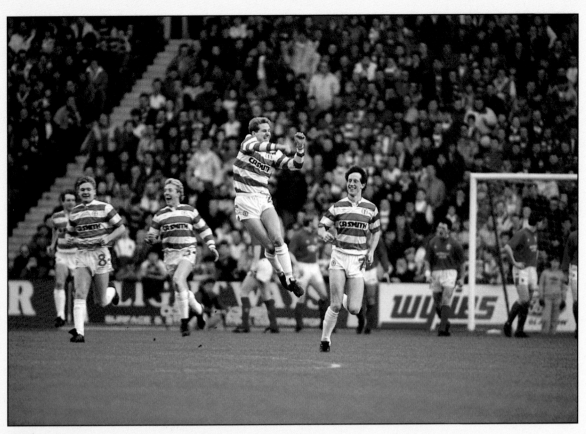

reaffirm their attitudes and values which they felt at pains to relate to their origins. It emphasised their lineage and the wholesome belief for example that no one man was more important than the club and it traditions. But it did not necessarily win football matches. Indeed looking back to that period when Celtic frequently agonised over such as the importance of playing for the colours above all else one cannot help but think of an Irishman perhaps less well known in the Parkhead 'Jungle' than Charles Patrick Tully, namely James Joyce, who once said, 'History is a subject from which I am still trying to wake up.'

The day Stein walked back through the door into a position of authority was the day Celtic football club departed from the semi-comatose contemplation of its own navel. The Bob Kelly autocracy had run out of steam. New ways had to be tried. It is interesting to note though that even to the end there was a reluctance to hand everything over to Stein. Stein told me quite distinctly in later years that the first offer to him was not to become outright manager of Celtic but to form a joint management team along with Sean Fallon. You could in the kindest analysis interpret this as simply part of the ritualistic *pas de deux* of negotiation but in any case Stein made it perfectly clear regardless of the risks of outright rejection that he could have none of that. It was then that Bob Kelly made the historic decision to make the final offer, no strings attached. The Protestant from Burnbank felt immediately at home in the manager's chair. It may have had traditions but he now had the power.

Celtic's first of two penalties. John Hughes ignores the fuss over the award. Ritchie ignores the ball

On the other side of the city, where traditional ways had worked successfully for more than two decades since the end of the war, Rangers seemed blissfully unaware of the changes seeping into the British game. If they were masters of all they surveyed then their vision was hardly twenty-twenty. When they ventured outside their own domain they seemed incapable of adapting from their own set ways of playing to the different standards of European football. Scot Symon, after all, the inheritor of the Struth tradition, had kept the ship in good order and apart from the occasional disappointment in Europe very few of the vast array of passengers who sailed with him showed any signs of mutiny, especially since during his management Rangers had beaten Celtic with a regularity that might have appeared tedious were it not for the fact that in Old Firm terms there is no such thing as the monotony of victory. They had the upper hand, they had the greater support, they had the money. What they did not have was foresight.

Symon was a visitor to training, not a participant. He was an impeccably dressed gentleman with a soft hat who, to the best of anybody's knowledge, never donned a track-suit in all his time as manager. His views on the game, as given to his players, were economical almost to the point of being furtive. His principal strength lay simply in being where he was as a manager of a club which could recruit the vast majority of the best talent in Scotland almost at the snap of a finger, but it is true that he backed that up by having a good eye for the promising player. Rangers could have been said to have been on auto-pilot at that time, with little perception of the storm clouds ahead or of the track-suit coming off the peg daily in the manager's office at Parkhead.

Stein's face when he presented himself there in 1965 was 'weel kent' among the players. They already knew something of his stature and personality, as John Clark colourfully recalls.

> Before he left to go to Dunfermline he was youth coach and I remember Billy McNeill and I were playing in the reserves one day and we were told to meet at Skinner's restaurant at one o'clock. We were early so we went for a walk. We got back to the restaurant at about one minute past one and Jock met us. He nearly went through us for not being on time. I remember standing there quaking. So when he came back to Parkhead as manager there was no way anybody was going to try him out on discipline and authority. Then almost as soon as he got back he took us all into the old gym in the stand and put up a blackboard and began to lecture us on tactics, chalking up all the moves and positions he wanted us in. We couldn't believe this compared to what used to go on. Every now and then he would get you to join in a discussion about tactics, but to be honest I cannot remember a single soul in my time who either disagreed with him or dared speak up about it. You just ended up believing that everything he told you would work out for us. And it almost always did, especially since he was so good in reading the opposition well. You got the impression he knew absolutely everything about every player that kicked a ball in Scotland. He missed nothing.'

He failed, though, at the first hurdle in his first Old Firm League game as manager, in the match at Ibrox a month before the League Cup Final when Jim Forrest unsettled Billy McNeill to great effect and the talented Rangers wingers Willie Henderson and Willie Johnston did more than anybody else to

carve out Rangers 2–1 victory. But in a sense, if it had given Stein more than a taste of what Rangers had to offer it had also revealed to him an underlying feeling of Celtic inferiority which made them feel that no matter how well they might play, because of the natural order of things Rangers would always end up on top. Bobby Murdoch, before Stein, had known the features of the wilderness like the back of his hand.

❝ Rangers just beat us at will most of the time. We couldn't seem to develop the same kind of confidence, not to say arrogance, that they had. We were young players and you always hoped that at some time in the future the tide would turn for the club. But at one stage I was so disillusioned I had almost packed my bags to go to Australia. I just couldn't see the way forward for Celtic. Then the Big Man arrived. All right, he talked tactics well and all that, but the most important thing was he just made the place buzz. Later on in my career I fell out with him because I knew he wanted to replace me with a running midfield player. I wasn't that; I was a passer of the ball. I left. But I can't really criticise because he really saved my career in the first place, and frankly he saved Celtic.'

---

23 October 1965	**Celtic 2 Rangers 1**	Hampden Park
	(League Cup Final)	

Celtic: Simpson, Young, Gemmell, Murdoch, McNeill, Clark, Johnstone, Gallagher, McBride, Lennox, Hughes

Rangers: Ritchie, Johansen, Provan, Wood, McKinnon, Greig, Henderson, Willoughby, Forrest, Wilson, Johnston

Scorers: (Hughes (18,28 – both pens.); Young (84, o.g.)

Referee: H.Phillips (Wishaw)   *att*: 107 609

The *pas de trois*. Bobby Lennox's head just stays on. Ronnie McKinnon sells a dummy to Billy Ritchie's fist. And Rangers survive heavy pressure

The Final on that Saturday, 23 October 1965, drew a record crowd for the League Cup of 107 609. As Jack Harkness wrote afterwards in the *Sunday Post*: 'It was a hard, grim game and it could be there are some who like their football this way. People who chew tobacco, bite their nails, eat razor blades, and that sort of thing.' You can sense the distaste in those words even at this distance. It reads almost like the weeping of a purist for a game that had debased itself. Harkness caught the mood of this game accurately, for by any interpretation of what happened that day it would be recalled for a level of nastiness that, even by Old Firm standards, made people cringe.

The tone was set in exactly two minutes when Celtic's right-back, Young, felled Willie Johnston. It was a crude tackle from which Johnston never fully recovered. Davy Provan makes no bones about his belief that the severity of the tackle was intentional.

> I'm not saying that Young was told to go out and kick Johnston, but I am convinced the motive was to try to make Johnston, who was possibly the fastest man on the park, less effective. He was "sorted out" as you might say. Managers don't need to tell players a deliberate ploy like that. But you can build up the right kind of attitude for it. There is no doubt in my mind that Johnston was targeted.'

John Clark disagrees.

> You can take it from me there was no talk in our dressing-room about sorting out anybody. It was a hard tackle right enough, but then no worse than I had seen in other Old Firm games. It came right at the start of the match and that's why people attached so much importance to it. Our instructions were

about playing football, about standing up to anything that Rangers would throw at us and using the great strengths we had on the wings. Certainly the Big Man had geed us up like nothing we had ever experienced before in an Old Firm game and we were in the right gear from the start, but nobody was to be singled out for any special "treatment".'

What the tackle did do was release certain inhibitions in virtually all of the players, and the game ended up with five being booked and the play distorted by an endless series of fouls, pulled jerseys, bickerings and raised fists. The game snarled its way to the first goal. John Clark had an ideal view of it.

> We were awarded a free kick. I placed the ball just inside their half and looked up towards the penalty area. Joe McBride, who was Jock's first signing, was standing with Ronnie McKinnon just behind him. I just lofted it, hoping I'd find Joe's head just inside the box. To my utter amazement I saw Ronnie McKinnon lift his hand and punch at the ball. I could hardly believe it. I'll bet the Rangers players couldn't either.'

Davy Provan hardly disagrees.

> You're right. I was still thinking it was a joke until big John Hughes stepped up and slotted the ball home from the spot. Can you imagine going down with a giveaway like that? But worse was to come and I was at the heart of it all. I was playing against Jimmy Johnstone and there is hardly any need to tell you that he was superb. Now despite what Celtic supporters might say, I will bet there is not one occasion when he went off the park having been deliberately kicked by me. The problem is when you are a big man like me playing against a wee fella like Johnstone, every tackle looks awkward. I think referees tend to over-protect the small player like that. Anyway, Jimmy was weaving his way into the penalty area and I tackled him. To me it was no better or worse than any of the other tackles I had made on him earlier, but he went down flat and all I can remember is the referee pointing to the penalty spot. It's never a nice feeling giving away a penalty. You can imagine what it was like in a Cup Final against Celtic. We protested about it, of course, but got nowhere. John Hughes did exactly the same and Celtic were two up with two penalties. It was grim. But I think what angered us most of all, and perhaps caused even worse feeling that day, was that in the second half Willie Henderson was brought down in the box by Tommy Gemmell by a tackle that was similar to mine, and the referee just waved play on. That was hard to take.'

It is better at this stage to separate the controversies over the handling of the game from the actual run of the play. The scribes of the day found this a difficult exercise, for while in general they felt Rangers had been hard done by in having the second penalty awarded against them and not being given a penalty themselves (to such an extent that Gair Henderson, writing in the *Evening Times*, said: 'In this final, apparently, sauce for the goose was not sauce for the gander'), they were as one in proclaiming Celtic's superiority in between these incidents, thus leading to the conclusion that their command of the match was scarcely reflected in a two-penalty-goal lead. John Hughes, who might have been the originator of the mystery tour idea because of the unpredictable paths he pursued on the field, got his geography exactly right that day and was running the legs off the Ibrox defence. Then, with a 2–0

John Greig suffers on the rack for scoring a goal that came just too late

lead and undoubted superiority, Celtic came out of the dressing-room after half-time and really proved that something special had come to Parkhead in the shape of Stein.

They proceeded to control the game by keeping within their sights the prime object of the exercise, which was to win the Cup. Not for Stein the desire to rub it in, or to allow Celtic players to be swayed by their superiority into reckless attacking against the Rangers barricades where too often previously they had perished. They guarded their lead. They did it in a way which suggested that a template for future European performances was being established, and which in retrospect was very much the way they played a European quarter-final tie away from home against Fiorentina five years later. The common sense that lay at the heart of the Stein philosophy was prevailing.

It seemed appropriate to their miserable day, then, that Rangers' goal six minutes from the end should have come from the head of a Celtic player when Ronnie Simpson palmed the ball against the back of Young's head and it ended up in the net. There was little danger of any more. When Hugh Phillips blew the whistle for full time he brought to an end a remarkable sequence of having refereed four finals in which Jock Stein had emerged the victorious manager, the other three being when Dunfermline had beaten Celtic to win the Scottish Cup, when Hibs had beaten Aberdeen to win the Summer Cup, and when Celtic had beaten Dunfermline to win the Scottish Cup a few months previously.

On this occasion, though, when Celtic came back on to the field to show the Cup to their supporters, there was an invasion from the Rangers end. It was mostly hundreds of young people who had flooded over the wall. Although they indulged in little more than scarf-waving, it looked more serious, although none of the Celtic players afterwards had felt any anxieties about it, as John Clark recalls.

They've won. Stein's first cup victory over his great opponents sparked off fury and resentment

> To be honest I had forgotten all about that. They did come on the park but none of us took it all that seriously. I remember one being pushed back by Tommy Gemmell as he rushed up to Billy McNeill, but maybe because we were still in a kind of elation about winning the Cup it didn't really bother us all that much.'

It bothered almost everyone else, and for days afterwards a debate raged as to the advisability of caging in supporters at games, and yet again the possibility of a ban on Old Firm matches was mooted – without there ever being a sensible proposal made as to how this would be feasible. In truth, most of the serious trouble happened outside the park. Joe McBride's shop in the Bridgeton area of the city had its windows broken. The Rangers team bus, stuck in a traffic jam at Crown Street in the Gorbals, was attacked and most of the windows smashed by bottles. The *Royal Ulsterman* made only a ten-minute trip up the Broomielaw in Glasgow before returning to its berth as Rangers and Celtic supporters clambered all over the boat in naval battles not witnessed since Errol Flynn sailed the Spanish Main.

A debate was initiated as to why Celtic had returned to the field of play with the Cup, as this was seen to be a provocation. To an outsider a team showing off the spoils of victory might not seem in the least unusual, but given the circumstances of this volatile atmosphere and the propensity to apportion blame one way or the other, solemn debate was held on this spontaneous act as if some form of outrage had been perpetrated. Celtic remained silent on this issue.

Coming off the field at the end Ronnie Simpson, tears flooding unashamedly down his cheeks, made a comment to a pressman which would turn out to be eerily prophetic: 'One day when the reflexes slow, the hands slip and the eye doesn't see the ball as big as a house, then the years will have won. But I hope there will be more triumphs with Celtic as long as they want me.' He was pointing, perhaps inadvertently, to something of significance that had happened that day and which, in the aftermath of discussion about violence among supporters, or raging arguments about penalties, was largely over-looked. This was the emergence of a much tougher Celtic, largely clued up in the ways of winning in this world and not prepared to be identified with that hopelessly romantic notion which had persisted for far too long that even if beaten by Rangers they had sometimes, after all, played the better football. The man in the track-suit had seen to that.

CHAPTER FIVE

DANISH BLUE

There was a time when the Scots were ill disposed towards welcoming Vikings to these shores. Normally at the slightest hint of their approach over the North Sea they would toll the warning bells and head for the hills, taking their goods and chattels with them – and hiding their women for good measure. Indeed, there is a monument at Largs to commemorate the extreme distaste the Scots had for this marauding race who felt the proud blow for Scottish independence on the Firth of Clyde in 1263. It took over seven centuries to dispel this revulsion, and the longboat being by then outmoded they returned by plane and settled principally in a place only half an hour from where their forefathers had been sent packing, Greenock. However attractive the Tail of the Bank may be to the foreigner, however, it was not as tourists that they came but as professional footballers, at the behest of one of the most colourful entrepreneurs in the business, Hal Stewart of Morton.

Hal almost single-handedly converted Scotland in the early 1960s to the view that the Scandinavians, particularly the Danes, did more than just make austere furniture and blue films. He colonised Greenock with men who sounded as if they were straight out of a Viking pageant: Sorensen, Johansen, Bertelsen, and others. They came to play football. And to the Danes, coming from an amateur scene in their own country, Greenock represented a kind of financial Valhalla. The Danish footballing diaspora which is now well enough known throughout Europe could be said to have started in Scotland through the instigation of the Greenock businessman who almost invariably wore a smart trilby and a luxurious smile.

His best deal might possibly have been the buying and eventual selling of a player by the name of Kaj Johansen. Johansen did not fit the normal mould of the tall blond Dane. He was relatively small, dark and fairly sallow. Neither was he exactly ugly, so both on and off the field his slight but athletic figure marked him out from others. In June 1965 Hal Stewart transferred Kaj Johansen to Rangers. Another full-back of the time, yet to reach the heights of his powers, was Tommy Gemmell, then embarking on his career with Celtic. Johansen meant nothing to him then, but in the fullness of time it was a name which was eventually to haunt him.

6 I swear to you that even now I can go into pubs and get into banter with Rangers supporters and some of them will shout out to me, "Well, what about Johansen then? What did he do to the Celtic then?" And these people are in their late teens or early twenties. They couldn't possibly have seen him play and they certainly would not have been at the game that made him famous. And yet they remember him and keep casting him up to me.'

The game which is indelibly stamped with the name of the Dane was the Scottish Cup Final replay of 27 April 1966.

Johansen had come to live in a country which seemed to have a lot to offer. Industry was booming, with manufacturing output up by 5 per cent on the previous year. Unemployment stood at its lowest in ten years at only 2.6 per cent and in the very week of that Final the *Glasgow Evening Citizen* was in the bountiful position of printing a large three-page spread packed tightly with adverts for jobs. And the *Scottish Daily Express* was reporting on a Glasgow family by the name of Donnelly who had emigrated to South Africa, then become stowaways on board a liner a few months later just to get back to the civilisation of 'fish-suppers and buttered-rolls'. Football, though, always proved an even stronger pull for the expatriate than those delicacies. That week they came from all over the world to see the two games, amassing an aggregate attendance over the Final and the replay, of 223 421.

Four days before the Final, Celtic had played Liverpool at Anfield in the second leg of the semi-final of the European Cup Winners' Cup. Their elimination gave rise to speculation as to how badly they might have been affected by that, considering they had been only one game away from a European Final which was to be played at Hampden Park itself. For anyone to have had any doubts about Celtic morale, however, was to be ignorant of the quality of Stein's control over the players. He kept them on mental alert by a mix of abrasion, impressively intuitive reading of the opposition and a brilliant wit which could be corrosive when required. It was highly unlikely that on their return from the game in England they had left their morale mashed on the Kop.

It was clear, though, that they were not without problems. They had thrashed Rangers 5–1 at Celtic Park the previous January, when Stein had shown his astuteness by having his players come on to the hard pitch before the game to try out a variety of studs, and as the Rangers players slithered about for the rest of the game the Celtic manager rammed home another example of how to out-think the opposition. But Rangers had caught them and were breathing down their necks in the League Championship race, having now drawn level with Celtic on points by beating Motherwell on the same evening as their great rivals were being eliminated from Europe. The long, hard season was beginning to take its toll, as Celtic fell into indecisiveness having failed to score more than one goal in their previous three games.

But one of the most significant factors in Celtic's League Cup victory over Rangers earlier that season had been the apparent vulnerability of Kaj Johansen against John Hughes. The Celtic winger, called affectionately 'Yogi' by those who were sometimes perplexed by his play, which had an unpredictable quality to it, had run the Dane into the ground with his pace and strength of possession, for he towered above most people on the field. It was a game which affected Johansen badly. His form evaporated over the next few months until he was uncertain of his place in the side. Scot Symon was hardly amused, and Johansen knew that.

> ❻   I knew I was capable of playing well in a good Rangers team, yet nothing
>   seemed to go right until the day the manager called us all to a meeting and
>   went to town on us. He told us we would have to improve quickly or drastic
>   measures would be taken. Immediately after the lecture by Mr Symon I went

upstairs to his office and had a long talk with him about my future with Rangers. And to his everlasting credit he listened to my side of the story and agreed to let me play my own type of game with John Greig in front of me. Back in the dressing-room I got together with the players and we discussed tactics and how to get the best possible value from the talent we had.'

He draws an extraordinary picture there of a club in crisis indulging in a kind of group-therapy exercise. Self-help seems to have been a major feature of Rangers' preparation at that time, as compared with the players of the club on the other side of the city who did not cross a touchline without various individual routes having been mapped out for them by the man in the dug-out. Symon, though, at this stage of his career seems to have been withdrawing more and more into a shell. He had never been an easily accessible man and the story is told of a journalist phoning him up with a question about the possible postponement of a game because of bad weather: 'Is there fog at Ibrox at the moment?' And after the characteristic hesitation, the reply came, 'No comment.'

On the other hand, Tommy Gemmell recalls the close talks he had with Stein.

They weren't so much overall tactics talks as trying to make you understand how well you could play yourself and what the opposition might have in store for you. He didn't often extol the virtues of the opposition because he obviously didn't want you to become obsessed by them. But he would talk to you about certain individuals, like Willie Henderson, for example. He'd tell you to try to keep Willie playing on his left side for he was hopeless there, and sure enough if you followed his advice you got results.'

DANISH
BLUE

51

Steve Chalmers put this one into the heavens. Celtic's hopes did not soar there in company

The two clubs met for the Final on Saturday 23 April in front of a crowd of 126 559. Celtic were expected to make most of the running, and they did. But they were capably matched by the Rangers defence which exhibited the tenacity of a set of players still hurt by their League Cup Final defeat of six months earlier. Making his début in an Old Firm game was lay preacher Bobby Watson.

❡ I was taken aside on the Wednesday and told I was playing in the Final. Then I was told I would be wearing the number eight jersey instead of the one I normally wore, number four. The manager just told me not to bother about the number, that it didn't really matter which jersey I wore. I couldn't quite grasp the significance of this because it wasn't really part of a new tactical switch for me as I was going to operate as usual in midfield in a 4–2–4 system which we used before it was actually recognised as such. But nothing more was added. We didn't discuss the game in any depth. I was wearing a different number and that was that. So out we went, determined to fight Celtic all the way because we now realised how fast their attack was and how well they would be prepared for us. I used to hate the sight of Bobby Lennox, for

Determination is writ large in the face of Ronnie Simpson as he punches his way out of trouble

example. I wasn't the fastest player in the world but I think he must have been close to it. I think Celtic owed a great deal to Lennox for the way he could take a ball from one end of the park to the other like a sprinter, so when we knew he wasn't actually playing in the match, no matter how well Hughes might play I considered Lennox's absence a bonus for us. Now we were mostly on the defensive but in actual fact we should have won the game because just before the end John Greig took off on a run, went right through the Celtic defence, pushed the ball to Johnston, got the return and swept it away from Simpson, but he dived to his left and just touched the ball away. It saved the game for Celtic.'

Tommy Gemmell remembers that save too, but feels if the ball had gone in it would have been a total injustice. Indeed, he feels a replay ought not to have been necessary.

❡ To be honest I thought we gave them a right going over in both games but couldn't put the ball in the net. We didn't feel down though, after that; in fact we were supremely confident we could take them in the second game.'

Between the games Bobby Watson felt he was in some kind of limbo.

❡ Remember this was my first season in the first team and I was only nineteen so I felt I needed some help, some advice. But I got nothing. You were really left on your own at Ibrox. Nobody said much which would help you to develop as a player. You just put a jersey over your head and got on with it. You had a natter with individual members of the side but it didn't really add up to significant coaching advice. I am convinced that young, promising talent

● **THE HERO OF HAMPDEN.** Kaj Johansen (left) makes himself the golden boy of Scottish soccer as he lashes the ball past Ronnie Simpson for Rangers' Scottish Cup winner. Celtic's beaten defenders are Bobby Murdoch, Tommy Gemmell and Billy McNeill.

was squandered as a result. So going into the second game I was just quite glad to know that I had so many experienced players beside me, like Jimmy Millar who'd been out of the team for some time but was brought back in to play in midfield.'

---

27 April 1966	**Rangers 1 Celtic 0**	Hampden Park

(Scottish Cup Final Replay)

Rangers: Ritchie, Johansen, Provan, Greig, McKinnon, Millar, Henderson, Watson, McLean, Johnston, Wilson

Celtic: Simpson, Craig, Gemmell, Murdoch, McNeill, Clark, Johnstone, McBride, Chalmers, Auld, Hughes

Scorer: Johansen (70)

Referee: T. Wharton (Clarkston)   *att*: 96 862

To the conqueror a handshake. John Hughes in a sporting gesture to Kaj Johansen who still can hardly believe his own triumph

Page 16 DAILY RECORD, Thursday, April 28, 1966

THE NIGHT KAJ

● THEIR HERO . . . Kaj Johansen is lifted shoulder high by the Rangers team. Skipper John Greig is about to be hoisted aloft, too.

The man who did so much...and lost

PAST cheering Rangers fans, Celtic manager Jock Stein (above) leaves Hampden last night. He has done so much for Celtic. He has seen them within sight of a European Cup victory over Liverpool and a Cup Final victory over Rangers. Both times his hopes were dashed but Jock won't give up so easily. On Saturday, Celtic can clinch the League title.

● WE DID IT! Wee Willie Henderson, smoking a celebration cigar, leaves Hampden.

● IT'S OURS! Rangers' b

SCORED GLORY GOAL

● It took a hard-fought minutes for Rangers put the ball into Celtic's goal . . . 16 minutes of skill, sweat, tension and se.

The forts had tried all they knew but still the goal escaped them.

It came the 70th minute of the Cup Final ay at Hampden last night.

. . . A it came from a completely unexpected re.

Kaj Johan the Dane who has never scored a goal Scotland, had decided he would never a better time.

Right-b Kaj flashed out of defence into the Celt penalty area and put the ball into the Celtel before anyone had time to ask what HE doing there.

★ ★

Hampdwent wild, the Rangers team jumped for and at the end hoisted their "defender" lder high.

It was only goal of the game that so many pe said Rangers would lose.

Rangerse underdogs, the team who had gone off so much that even their own fans were ding a Cup Final with Celtic, had done it in.

And Ka Even if he never scores again, fans will be ing about his glory goal in 1976 . . . after.

Pictures of the ame and the scenes which followed were taken by cord's camera team . . . Bill Brown, Bert Paterson, n Campbell, George McEwan, Eric Craig, Allon and Robert Hotchkiss.

captain John Gret the cup in triumph last night.

● THE BATTLE'S O'ER . . . Johnston and Watson of Rangers have played themselves almost to a standstill, but now the game is over and they have won. Months of training, many a close-fought victory, then a drawn game and at last success. Laughing, they congratulate each other in a moment they will never forget.

DANISH BLUE

57

The Wednesday evening turned out to be mild but windy. This time there were 96 862 inside Hampden to watch Celtic kick off against the sun and wind. To read any account of that game nowadays is to try to unravel the mystery of Celtic's defeat. The statistics tell a story of Celtic dominance in attack and astonishing misses in front of goal. With the score 0–0 at half-time and Celtic now to play with the strengthening wind at their backs, they expected some dividend from their pressure. All they got was a dose of acute frustration as Rangers, especially through Willie Henderson, relied on quick breakaways and in so doing began to appear more likely to score despite the greater Celtic pressure. Tommy Gemmell began to worry.

> A year later when we were playing in the Final of the European Cup in Lisbon I actually thought back to the night at Hampden when we hit Rangers with everything and couldn't score. In Lisbon just before I scored I was beginning to think that we were going to suffer the same fate. Well, everybody now knows what happened in Lisbon well enough [they beat Inter Milan 2–1 to win the European Cup], but at Hampden that night, as the game went into the second half, I have to admit I just couldn't see us scoring. We kept plugging away but there was something missing up front. We just weren't snappy enough.'

The scoring of the only goal of the game came in such a spectacular way and from such an unusual source that one can only look upon it as something akin to the perfect punch thrown in a classical manner by a boxer who has spent his time in the ring using the ropes to elude an opponent swinging wildly at him. The Dane, having stood his ground more confidently this time against Hughes, had already ventured forward earlier in the game and had a shot blocked. Then, twenty minutes from the end, he encountered the ball in a manner that could have been described as magnificent stealth. Johansen came from nowhere.

> I honestly cannot remember just how Willie Johnston took the ball to the by-line before crossing. But I do recall George McLean just failing to make contact with Willie's cross. Then Willie Henderson crashed in a first-timer that was blocked. When the ball broke to me I think John Hughes and I were the only players outside the Celtic penalty area, apart from Billy Ritchie and possibly Ronnie McKinnon. As soon as I saw it coming in my direction I made up my mind to go right for it.
>
> The ball was bouncing awkwardly but I controlled it with the inside of my foot before taking a quick step and hitting it while it was still a foot or so off the ground. And I really met that ball squarely with my instep. But I had no thoughts of aiming for the near post although the far side of the goal was crammed with players. The one message that kept flashing through my brain was "Keep it low! Keep it low!" And I did. For a second I thought Ronnie Simpson had stopped it – then I saw the ball spin round the back of the net and my heart stopped.
>
> In all my years in senior football I had never shown any emotion. I had never hugged a player, never even leapt in the air. But at that moment I just couldn't help it.'

They smothered Johansen, for even though there were still twenty minutes left the shot from about 22 yards had such an appearance of stunning finality about it that the Rangers players gave way to an elation that was heavily spiced with enormous relief. The Rangers supporters who had watched their team with their backs against the wall for so long in the match rent the night with such a roar that it might have been heard in Johansen's native country. A new hero had been born, and if he were to do nothing else for the club the Rangers supporters would remember his name affectionately for succeeding generations. The game was won, despite some Celtic attacks which came near to producing an equaliser but were too frantic to pierce a Rangers defence which had once again proved that if you show resolution then sometimes you will also get the break of the ball.

A Celtic player and fellow countryman, Bent Martin, babysat for Johansen while he and his wife and the Rangers party went off to celebrate at the St Enoch hotel. They were not to know as they popped the champagne just how momentous that game had been. Celtic, even in defeat, had delivered a message which eluded most people that night. The dramatic eruption of the winning goal had obscured the true nature of the game, which had been one of Celtic dominance. Rangers had won by a mixture of improvisation and unquenchable pride in their colours, as typified by their veteran player Jimmy Millar, who had been brought back into the team specially for the Final and, according to Gair Henderson of the *Evening Times*, played so well that 'the Celtic players must have thought there wasn't just one Jimmy Millar but triplets'. But it was a triumph which hardly registered as a guide to the future.

Celtic, on the other hand had failed, but in such a manner as to suggest that they were a new force gathering a momentum which was not far short of full acceleration. But nobody paid much attention to that because a Dane had captured the evening, and in the ensuing thunderous acclaim Rangers simply could not hear the alarm bells sounding for them.

Scot Symon 'captured' by delighted supporters and revealing a rare public smile

CHAPTER SIX

QUALITY CONTROL

T
he sacking of Scot Symon was brutal if only because they tried to make it seem so civilised. He was invited to see the Glasgow accountant Alec McBain one afternoon in October 1967 outside of Ibrox, little realising what was in store. He may not have been unaware of the growing anxieties of the Rangers supporters about the ability of the club to meet the Celtic challenge. But then, at that juncture Rangers were top of the League and unbeaten. In banking terms you might have said that on current account Symon's balance was good. There was no cause to expect anything other than a social reason for the invitation to the accountant's home. It was much less innocuous than that, however. After a few minutes of introductory pleasantries, he was out of a job. He had been told, extremely politely, that Rangers Football Club no longer required his services. It still seems particularly insensitive that this pleasant acquaintance of Symon's was used as an emissary by the Ibrox board, which simply exposed itself to the accusation that it was dodging the issue. Even Symon's critics felt it discredited the club.

It was clear that Ibrox was in the early stages of what might be described as the 'Stein dementia'. They were now beginning to appreciate that the club was faced by a man of immense managerial ability who was beginning to dominate not only the game but the media as well, thus lifting Celtic to the kind of status previously enjoyed only by Rangers. The early nerves about this were giving way to a condition approaching panic.

The embarrassing defeat at Berwick 1–0 in the Scottish Cup in January of 1967 had wounded the club in a way that almost irrevocably scarred their pride. And they had not yet solved the perennial problem of how to cross the Channel and play successfully in Europe. After Celtic won that year in Lisbon, Rangers slumped in Nuremberg with a team selection which drove mild-mannered chairman John Lawrence to convene a press conference on the eve of the game, deploring the number of half-backs in the forward line. There were any number of reasons why Scot Symon would have had to be extremely myopic not to have realised that his oak-panelled and ample office at the head of the marble stairs was not also going to be his eventide home.

And yet when the time of departure arrived in late 1967 there were hardly any who did not suffer a sense of surprise and shock because of the manner in which it was done, and also because his name seemed irrevocably associated with the lineage of the club and the dynastic mould of imperious Rangers managers. Symon was a complex figure who could be both aloof and arrogant but also extremely dignified and courteous, although he did give the impression in his heyday at Ibrox that he regarded the press in general as a renegade bunch of saboteurs and seemed to enjoy having them wait on the doorstep of the club in both the literal and metaphorical sense. On the Saturday after his sacking, to sum him up as a man and as a football manager the BBC chose to interview one of his ex-players, Ian McMillan. The 'Wee Prime Minister' was always considered one of the fairest sportsmen in the land; his loudest oath ever on the field was thought to be the day he told an opponent to 'go away and pee'.

Suddenly during the interview he launched into attack on Symon, not in intemperate language but in a more effectively cool and clinical dissection of the man and his cripplingly inadequate grasp of modern tactics. He cited in graphic detail the Eintracht Frankfurt away leg in the semi-final of the European Cup in 1960 when at half-time the score was a creditable 1–1. But McMillan went on:

> Frankly the writing was on the wall. They had hit the post several times, the cross-bar twice, and George Niven in goal had made some superb saves. Yet when we went back into the dressing-room at half-time with some real thinking to be done about this, the manager offered us nothing but just went on drinking his cup of tea. There we were being hammered, lucky still to be alive, and nothing being offered in the way of how we might regroup our defence. We went back out on to the park to improvise and were obliterated. We lost five goals in the second half and there is little doubt that the manager had to accept a great deal of the responsibility for sending us out to play the same way as we might have against Airdrie in the Scottish League. There was no way Rangers could go on like that any longer.'

Even though he had expressed himself in his usual mild-mannered way, the extent of the attack on Symon was astonishingly effective in light of the sympathetic press which the ex-manager had had over the manner of his dismissal. McMillan, speaking with the authority of a player, and a loyal player at that, of great standing, had put the sacking into its proper perspective. But it hurt. Some days later on the way to a midweek game in Dundee I stopped over for a sandwich at the Isle of Skye hotel in Perth and walked straight into Scot Symon sitting having tea overlooking the river. I greeted him and asked him politely if he was going to the game in Dundee. He looked me straight in the eye and with a very thin and withering smile he said, 'If my wife had got her hands on you on Saturday night she would have torn your eyes out for the interview you did with McMillan.' Then he paused, obviously enjoying the discomfort I felt at having the wind taken out of my sails. But then, in a sudden recovery of the dignity which was to manifest itself more keenly in his later years with Partick Thistle, he drew himself up in his seat and added, 'But this is neither the time nor the place to discuss the matter. I hope you enjoy the game tonight.'

The extreme politeness at the end of the brief encounter did more than the original rebuke to make me feel guilty, as if somehow I had been party to an unwarranted assassination of his character. But at the same time, without the power of his great managerial post he looked, if not a broken man, at least an extremely fragile one, realising perhaps that people would not in future be hanging on his every word.

So Davy White, thirty-five years of age, lately of Clyde and upgraded to assistant manager at Ibrox, was further elevated into the managerial chair and left to face Jock Stein. In one of their first meetings, at a reception some weeks later at the BBC studios, Stein, who had heard that White did not want to appear in a joint interview with the Celtic manager because he feared he might be roasted alive, went out of his way to assure him that his fears were unfounded. I listened to him as he heartily explained that it was out on the field that he would try to embarrass him, not in a television studio. I could not help but feel, though, that Jock Stein was enjoying all of this and that he was in effect patronising the younger man whom deep down he knew he could eat for breakfast.

In fact, in his first season, despite the reservations about his appointment which hung around him for a while like a thick fog, White displayed determination and then went boldly into the transfer market in late 1968 to buy Colin Stein from Hibs (who in a mere two games became something of a cult figure among the Rangers supporters who had not seen anyone in a blue jersey score two consecutive hat-tricks) and St Johnstone player Alec Mac-Donald (who was to become one of the most influential but publicly under-rated players Rangers possessed in that era). They carried the Championship campaign right through to the final match of the 1967–68 season, and only a defeat at home against Aberdeen cost them the title. But the sorely tried supporters were in no mood to extend tolerance for ever, and the following season when Celtic began to leave Rangers well behind, the blue legions headed for Hampden Park on 26 April 1969 for the Scottish Cup Final against Celtic not just as support to the club but also as a massive jury about to declare judgement.

| 26 April 1969 | Celtic 4   Rangers 0 | Hampden Park |
| | (Scottish Cup Final) | |

Celtic: Fallon, Craig, Gemmell, Murdoch, McNeill, Brogan (Clark), Connelly, Chalmers, Wallace, Lennox, Auld

Rangers: Martin, Johansen, Mathieson, Greig, McKinnon, D. Smith, Henderson, Penman, Ferguson, Johnston, Persson

Scorers: McNeill (2), Lennox (44), Connelly (45), Chalmers (75)

Referee: J. Callaghan (Glasgow)   *att*: 132 874

Celtic, meanwhile, were relatively unconcerned. Although they had lost three out of their last five meetings with Rangers before this Final, they were going through a phase in which it was felt that when it really mattered they would produce the goods. Faith, anyway, in the manager Jock Stein was absolute and where you have faith you have ritual, an essential part of which seemed to be Seamill on the Clyde coast before big games. Jim Craig was in the squad.

> Frankly, we went to Seamill because Big Jock liked going there himself. I didn't see any tremendous value in it except that for some of the married men it meant maybe getting away from screaming weans for a couple of days. But Jock liked the company and the banter and it seemed to help him because he was tense before these games. But he knew when to make himself felt. On the morning of the Final I was sitting having breakfast when he came

in and shoved a morning newspaper under my nose and said "Read that!" Basically, the preview of the game by Willie Waddell had said that I would be vulnerable to the speed of the big Swede, Persson. "Read that and go out and stuff that report down his throat." That sort of approach gave you the right edge. And I must admit that within the first minute on the park I found myself wiring into Persson and, looking back, I think I did go over the top a bit. But if I had allowed him to dictate the kind of game to me that he liked he would have had a field day.'

John Greig, Rangers' captain, has good cause to look back on the second minute of that game as an unmitigated disaster.

> To be honest, in those days we always felt that we were playing twelve men: the eleven Celtic players and Jock Stein. He seemed to think up something new every time we played them. So before this one we talked through our tactics carefully. Now whatever else might have been said about him, Davy White knew the game well. He had a sound grasp of tactics and he talked a lot of sense about how to play a match. We thought we were well prepared. We had worked out in particular about how to defend at set pieces. Billy McNeill was always going to be a threat in the air in our penalty area. So Alec Ferguson, who had come into the team because Colin Stein had been suspended, was appointed to mark Billy whenever he moved up field. In the second minute they got a corner on our right which was taken by Bobby Lennox. To say something went wrong with our marking is an understatement. Alec Ferguson told me later something distracted him in the penalty area. Whatever it was, Billy McNeill rose up with an almost free header and stuck it past Norrie Martin. Now if you lose a goal like that so early, all the tactical preparation for the rest of the game can go for nothing. They had taken the initiative when we thought we would be upsetting them with Ferguson to worry McNeill and Willie Johnston going through gaps. Instead it had all happened in reverse. It was an enormous psychological blow.'

Under normal circumstances losing an early goal in a Cup Final can precipitate a nervous breakdown among even the hardiest of souls. It says something for Rangers that in this most bitterly contested match, and with the most carefully thought-out tactics the club had ever indulged in, and after having lost a goal that would have embarrassed a churches' league team, they came back at Celtic – only to find that a man whom even the most ardent Celtic supporter thought at the time to be a very fragile last-defence goalkeeper, John Fallon, had discovered his hands again and made a significant and brilliant save when he dived to his left to stop a fierce shot from Persson. Shortly after that he swooped to push out a shot from Greig, only to watch Ferguson fall over the ball when it looked easier to score. Ten minutes later Henderson ran in on goal and with only Fallon to beat ballooned the ball over the bar. But in truth, although these are the statistics of missed chances, sometimes you find in a game that a team playing, as Rangers then were, with some spirit are nevertheless less in control of themselves than the opposition who are operating at a less frantic level but building the basis for ultimate control. In between these hectic Rangers flurries Celtic were playing, understandably with their early one-goal lead, with a composure exemplified by George Connelly who, although ostensibly in as a substitute for the suspended Jimmy Johnstone, was operating in midfield with that deceptive calm which might have appeared

John Fallon smothers a shot. The defenders do not suffer shock at the sight

The early clash between Craig and Johnston. There was a marked absence of fraternal exchanges

Bobby Lennox looks as if he has accomplished a fine task scoring Celtic's second goal. Ronnie McKinnon looks as if he's seen a ghost

Many defenders, few attackers, and John Fallon leaps highest of all

innocuous compared with all the flailing of limbs that was going on around him, in an increasingly nasty game, but one which for all that carried the seeds of Rangers' imminent destruction.

John Greig was in fact beginning to grow in optimism.

And then it happened. We were about ninety seconds or so away from getting into the dressing-room for a half-time talk that I think would have helped a great deal, when Persson tried a short square pass to Mathieson. But it was too careless and George Connelly intercepted and just poked it through to Bobby Lennox. He was totally uncovered. Off he went at that great speed of his. Nobody could catch him. He swept the ball inside Norrie Martin's right-hand post and we were two down. If you think that was a gift it was nothing to what was to follow. Just seconds after that came what I think must be the most embarrassing moment in my whole playing career. I still can hardly credit it. Our goalkeeper played a short goal-kick to me. I think I was only half prepared for it. Anyway, I played it far too casually and tried to poke it back to him but muffed it and George Connelly stepped in, accepted the gift and strolled past Martin with the ball, as easy as you like. And I had done all that at the Celtic end, too. It was murder to bear, I can tell you.'

So Celtic went in at half time 3–0 up and in a state of delirium combined with incredulity, for while they had been controlling the flow of the game they had been handed gifts of such magnitude that if they had contracted the opposition to lie down and surrender half-way through the game their great rivals could not have done so with such creative aplomb. As Jim Craig remembers, Stein tried to keep them in check.

> During the whole of the interval he kept telling us to keep calm and that in an Old Firm game you never knew what might happen. But he was finding it difficult himself to believe that, because there wasn't anybody there who didn't think the Cup was well and truly won. It was like the end of the game in many ways.'

It wasn't, in fact. Fifteen minutes from the end of the match Steve Chalmers broke away on a solo run and fired in a shot which went into the net between Norrie Martin and the near post. This fine goal acted as the coda to a game of unequals. Rangers merely confirmed the view that Stein held sway in a manner which affected not merely the Ibrox tactical thinking, of which there had been much for this game, but more particularly their psychological make-up. They had approached this game with the nervous uncertainty of inferiors, and played as such. White was clearly no match for Stein in firming attitudes before the game and it could be said that the incredible mistakes made by talented players sprang from a lack of self-confidence, of which there was an abundance in that period at Ibrox. Tactical know-how was seen to be irrelevant if it were applied without conviction. White, however talented he had been in reading a game, had merely contrived to make Jock Stein look even bigger. There wasn't a Rangers supporter who left Hampden that day who did not believe that David White's days were numbered as manager of the club and that the sacking of Scot Symon, while in many ways justified, had merely created for Ibrox a new set of problems. However much they tried Rangers could not find a way to end the Stein era, which had now given Celtic access not just to triumph but also to plunder.

Close marking by Brogan of Celtic on Henderson of Rangers. The ball proves elusive

CHAPTER SEVEN

THE LIKELY LAD

lthough they discovered oil in the North Sea in 1970, the news was hardly the major currency of conversation among teenagers in Scotland, who might well have been more engrossed in contemplating the heights of hemlines, for the mini was enjoying a certain vogue, or in the cultivation of fashionably long hair at a time when sidelocks clung to male faces like gathering moss. Youngsters sat in cafés and listened to Lee Marvin singing 'I Was Born Under a Wandrin' Star', which Rangers supporters were to parody in words which re-sited the Yukon in Ulster, or they were entranced by the throbbing tones of Elvis Presley whose 'Wonder of You' stayed in the charts for twenty weeks. They were also amused by a song called 'Back Home', sung by a certain group of English footballers bound for Mexico and the World Cup. Nobody north of the border shared its optimism.

The North Sea to most of them was a blue expanse on the wall map in the geography class. Or, in teenage Derek Johnstone's case, it was those waters which lay close to his home in Dundee and which sent the stingingly cold winds to rebuke the masses of young footballers who learned their craft on the many city pitches on Saturdays. As a sixteen-year-old with a physique and ability well beyond his years, it was not too surprising that, as for most of us, the news of a potentially new industrial era dawning under the cruel sea meant little to him, and that he was much more excited about the fact that he was being called up to become a professional footballer with Rangers. That year, in the honoured tradition of the pioneer, the young man went west. There was nothing much of current value for him to see in the trophy room at the stadium for the club had failed to win a trophy since 1966. Indeed, the only solid challenge to Jock Stein and Celtic had come from the rather taciturn man from the north, Eddie Turnbull the then manager of Aberdeen, who in May that year had wrested the Scottish Cup from Stein.

Rangers during that period could not grasp the full reality of meaningful change and were still unable to understand that the surgeon's knife was needed rather than the beautician's palette. Events pressurised them, however, and with the humiliating defeat by Gornik in the Cup Winners' Cup and stories of indiscipline among the players on the eve of the match, David White was sacked as manager in November 1969. The man with whom the supporters wanted to replace him, according to a poll in the *Scottish Daily Express*, was Willie Waddell who, of course, wrote for that newspaper.

Shortly before the White sacking, on the night before Scotland's decisive World Cup match against West Germany in Hamburg in 1969, Waddell spent a convivial evening in my company along with the late John Fairgrieve, then with the *Daily Mail*, and the Scottish Football Association doctor. With the speculation about his possible appointment to Rangers intensifying by the hour, Waddell stated unequivocally to us that under no circumstances would he accept an offer to go to Ibrox. Indeed, he got rather heated about the suggestion. On Wednesday 3 December he took the job. In retrospect, I believe at that moment he was spontaneously registering his disgust at a club which in so many ways had lost its identity and, indeed, in several instances its dignity. It was the trend he was rejecting, not the club, for when the call eventually came it proved irresistible.

Despite his experience as a journalist, even he must have been taken aback by the press reaction which, had it been turned to music, would have sounded something like the 'Hallelujah Chorus'. That he was seen as some kind of saviour was hardly surprising, because there was no one else on the horizon capable of matching the stature of Jock Stein, who not only outfoxed Rangers most times on the field but also out manoeuvred them off it as well.

Waddell was faced by a master propagandist who could capture a headline with an ease which might have been the envy of the most sophisticated public relations expert. In his spare time Stein could have held night classes in psychology. To my knowledge he had not studied Freud or Kraft-Ebbing, or even John Le Carré, yet he gave the impression that he understood the human condition better than most and knew when necessary how to exploit people to the maximum. Sometimes he did it ruthlessly, sometimes with subtlety, but always with cunning. In being prepared for the daily battle to command attention for his club he had the distinct advantage of having crossed the social divide from his strongly Protestant background to Celtic Park, and he was acutely aware of the historical advantages Rangers had enjoyed through the years. He worked so diligently at influencing the minds of the people in the media that an unprecedented tension was created. There had been some stimulating relations between managers and the media prior to Stein arriving on the scene, but none to equal his scale of involvement where virtually every editor in the land had been taken to task in varying degrees for articles or broadcasts, some of which might not even have been connected with Celtic but simply with Scottish football as a whole. All this had the premeditated effect of making him universally respected and occasionally feared .

Tommy Gemmell, the flamboyant full-back whom Stein liked but with whom he had certain conflicts, was fully aware of his manager's influence.

> I really did get the impression that Jock got out a ruler every morning and measured the inches given to Celtic and Rangers coverage, and if *they* got more, somebody somewhere was in for it. He would invent stories just to make sure he got a headline and get everybody geed up in the week of an important game. I used to train every Sunday morning on my own at Parkhead and I can remember he had the press in his office at the same time. I tell you this, some of the bollockings I heard him give the press were unbelievable. He was really the first manager, I think, who knew the importance of using the press, and by God he did it in a big way.'

Waddell knew what he was up against and he hardly needed reminding that red, white and blue scarves were being taken out of the cupboards again throughout the land by those who were, until his appointment, seriously beginning to contemplate taking up shopping as a Saturday recreation. My first interview with him in the week of his appointment was like talking to an advocate given the brief of defending someone caught with a hand in the till. His terse outline of his views were realistic, economical and devoid of blethering optimism. He was offering no panacea, but his very stern and powerful presence in the stadium was enough to convince you that he felt he would find the solution and that the patient was not in such a hopeless condition as you might have thought. Two weeks later he was on the phone complaining bitterly about what he thought was a distorted report by one of our correspondents at the game. The battle with Stein for the minds of the people had truly been joined.

Almost a year later, however, Rangers under Waddell had won nothing, and indeed on the Saturday before the League Cup Final of 1970 Aberdeen had shown too much guile for them at Ibrox and had beaten them 2–0 hardly breaking sweat. At that moment, despite the respect he commanded among the supporters, he must have realised that with nothing to show for all his efforts his credibility was on the line.

---

24 October 1970   **Rangers 1   Celtic 0**   Hampden Park
                    (League Cup Final)

Rangers: McCloy, Jardine, Miller, Conn, McKinnon, Jackson, Henderson, Mac-Donald, D. Johnstone, Stein, Johnston

Celtic: Willams, Craig, Quinn, Murdoch, McNeill, Hay, J. Johnstone, Connelly, Wallace, Hood (Lennox), Macari

Scorer: D. Johnstone (40)

Referee: T. Wharton (Glasgow)   *att*: 106 263

On the face of it, it certainly was not the most auspicious time in the history of the club to bring in a sixteen-year-old boy to become the youngest-ever Cup finalist. Yet the day before the Final Derek Johnstone was taken into the boot room by Waddell and the assistant manager Jock Wallace and told he was going to play the following day. He was handed his quota of Cup Final tickets as if he was coming of age and the game was his sort of bar mitzvah. He went back that night to his bed and dreamed of scoring the winner.

> I honestly did. I know it's easy to say that now but I actually could see myself scoring the winner. I suppose every player does before a big game. But I dreamed about it and I actually slept well because I hadn't taken in what was happening to me. I just hadn't had enough time to think it all through, and anyway at my age I suppose I just wasn't old enough to be aware of the terrifying pressure surrounding a Cup Final. No, I cannot recall being a bit nervous, even right up to kick-off.'

Harry Hood, who was to become the highest scorer in the Celtic side that season, was in the rather bemused Celtic dressing-room three paces away from where Rangers were stripping for action.

> "Who's Derek Johnstone?" That's what we were all asking. Nobody had ever heard of him. Somebody thought he was a young lad but we couldn't tell his

Johnston's speed causes
exasperation to Craig

age, although we thought he had made his début against Cowdenbeath a few weeks previously. This did our morale no harm at all considering we had just heard as well that John Greig wasn't playing. We couldn't believe our luck that he had been passed unfit for the match, because to be honest nobody under-rated John's influence with Rangers. In fact, you could have said he *was* Rangers, because he had done a lot to hold them together. I don't know what they were thinking in their dressing-room but we couldn't have felt better getting that sort of news. Now having said that, some people have often said that Celtic, as hot favourites to win and with Rangers fielding a side without Greig, and with a teenager playing against one of the best centre-halves in the business in Billy McNeill, must have treated it all too lightly. But you just never took an Old Firm game lightly.'

Alec MacDonald reveals that Rangers in fact felt in fine fettle.

We had faith in the boss and we knew that this big lad had the right temperament. Anybody of his age who could stick into John Greig at training and knock him about a bit was obviously not going to be overawed by Billy McNeill. Certainly we were going to miss John Greig, but as I recall it nobody was depressed. Indeed, that morning at Ibrox we had gone in to have hot baths and followed that up by being hosed down with ice-cold water by Jock Wallace, who was assistant manager then. It doesn't seem important to anybody else but I think we just caught the right kind of aggressive mood there and then with the Big Man bashing us about with water in the baths. And we always knew that attitude was going to be even more important than team selection.'

It was wet at Hampden, too. The rain fell steadily on a crowd of 106 263 which, as the whistle went, had habitually forgotten portents, current form and the statistical advantage of Celtic who were aiming for their sixth League Cup Final win in a row. Rangers without Greig had changed their tactics to a 4–2–4 system with Alec MacDonald partnering the eighteen-year-old Alfie Conn, whose precocity fitted perfectly with the aggressive industry of his older partner. They took the game to Celtic using the running strengths of their wingers Willie Johnston and Willie Henderson, whose erratic talent had lain dormant far too often since the days when he first burst upon the scene as a youthful prodigy; but that day he was the equal of Jimmy Johnstone who, like too many of the Celtic players, simply could not get into proper gear.

And in the double-spearheading attack, beside the experienced Colin Stein, was the teenager from Dundee who looked so nerveless that the match might well have been played at Broughty Ferry in his own back yard. Derek Johnstone remembers:

Determination from Billy McNeill and Alfie Conn. The winner is goalkeeper Williams

> Nerveless? I think I just felt nothing. The occasion was so big that I couldn't take it all in. I know that I beat big Billy in the air several times early on because the balls fell short of him, and that helped, of course. I had Colin Stein beside me and we were getting good crosses from 'Bud' Johnston and Willie Henderson, men who were just big names to me when I was at school just six months previously. Cup Final? It honestly just felt like any other game of football.'

The innocence of youth translated itself into one climactic moment five minutes before half-time. Johnstone moved towards the edge of the penalty box.

> I remember Alec MacDonald starting off the move. He sent Willie Johnston away on the right wing. At first I was surprised to see Willie on that side of the field where Willie Henderson had started off, but as he went forward I tried to position myself away from the defence. The ball when it came across was actually well hit. As I recall it didn't drift in. It came between Jim Craig and Billy McNeill. There might just have been a bit of hesitation between the pair of them but I jumped and can remember turning my head towards goal as the ball hit it.'

The ball went from side of head to wet surface and shot past Evan Williams, the Celtic goalkeeper, twelve yards away and nestled in the right-hand corner of the net. Alec MacDonald's admiration naturally knew no bounds.

> I still call it the "Good Morning" Derek Johnstone header. That's the way I describe it to players to this day when I'm talking about the simple way you can nod your head and glide the ball towards the net, given the right kind of cross. It was beautifully taken and all the more remarkable for such an inexperienced player.'

Harry Hood gives full credit to Johnstone for the goal.

> You could say he wasn't covered properly; you might say that the ball skimmed quickly over the greasy surface; but at the end of the day it was a great leap and superbly directed header. He was against a great jumper for the ball and a goalkeeper on form, so in no way could it have been considered a flukey affair, certainly not in looking back to the kind of headed goals Johnstone was to score continually later in his career.'

One down at the interval, it was natural that Celtic would come out and lift their game, given the intensity of a Jock Stein lecture at half-time. But this contained nothing of the kind of relentless pursuit of victory which had characterised the side in the previous season. The European Cup Final defeat in Milan by Feyenoord, where Stein had grossly underestimated the opposition and where the old disciplines of painstaking preparation for the game had been compromised by the introduction of a players' agent who was as much in evidence as the manager himself before the Final, seemed to have debilitated Celtic to an extent. The customary hunger and bite were lacking as Rangers began to re-create some of the superior attitude, and skills to match, which they hadn't demonstrated since the early days of Symon.

Celtic certainly had their moments, particularly through Bobby Murdoch whose free kicks in the second half bothered the Rangers defence; and when the same player beat four men inside the box and laid the ball back for Wallace to blast it over from six yards, it was typical of the day for them. A goal then would have been an injustice, for Rangers had dominated most of the game and perhaps the hardest-working player of all on the day, Colin Stein, with four minutes to go, had the frustration of seeing a shot hit the inside of the far post and rebound along the line into goalkeeper Evan Williams' arms.

Then Willie Johnston sat on the ball. Harry Hood concedes:

> We certainly didn't like that. In fact, it incensed us. We had beaten Rangers

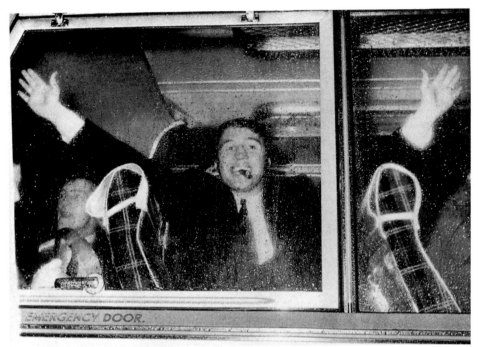

EMERGENCY DOOR.

regularly, and in Cup Finals sometimes handsomely, but we had never taunted them the way Bud did to us that day. I remember meeting him at a charity do not long after and I told him some Celtic players were so annoyed that he was a marked man. I never thought he played a single good game against Celtic after that.'

It was a minor blemish on a game that Rangers deserved to win against all the odds. The noises coming from the Rangers end were a mixture of ecstasy and relief.

Of course, it could be said that Rangers engaged in a terrifying gamble in fielding such a young player. But set against the general run of play their win was as much based on tactical good sense as it was on playing a hunch. While Jock Wallace was dispensing bear hugs to all and sundry and thereby endangering the lives of several players at the finish, Willie Waddell acted with more restraint because he knew that people might read too much into this victory. He had stabilised Ibrox and won back the faithful, but he knew there was more hard work to be done to lift Rangers to the European level he desired. But hard to please though he was, he must have indulged in some quiet gloating in having unveiled a new star in such an historic way.

Derek Johnstone had no time to celebrate, for he went to Iceland to play for the Scottish Professional Youth team. There in Reykjavik he lost his precious Cup Winner's medal; on his return he shamefacedly told Willie Waddell. On the telephone command of the Rangers manager the Icelanders mounted something like a nationwide search for the little piece of metal. When it was eventually unearthed, the teenage Johnstone must have regarded it as a much more important find than that dark gooey stuff they had discovered under the waters not far from his native city.

Consenting adults. Willie Henderson about to survive a hug from a delighted Jock Wallace

CHAPTER EIGHT

ONE WINTER'S DAY

T he turn of the year stirs the collective emotions probably more than at any other time in Scotland. At Hogmanay we have claimed almost proprietorial rights to that emotional juggling act that has us toss around nostalgia and expectation until one or both disappear in the wee sma' hours of New Year's morning. Dealing with that state of spiritual and physical exhaustion on 1 January is an art form which few master, and the majority are sometimes led to the doleful conclusion that perhaps total abstinence has something going for it after all. On that day most of us are generally in need of repair and go our various ways in search of it.

The most virile trail of all has led in the past to the Old Firm Ne'erday game. This fixture, now a movable feast, fitted in as naturally to the New Year celebrations as a cork does to a vintage wine, and in keeping with the nature of the season the uncorking of that bottle seemed the most indispensable ritual of winter. This seemed particularly so when, as a youngster shivering with cold and enclosed in balaclava and scarf, you were lifted over the turnstiles and helped up the steps to the rim of the terraces from where you had to worm your way to an air pocket in the midst of a phalanx of adult bodies. We stood on tiptoe and fervently believed that doing so aided growth better than taking orange juice. Never at any time, either in the occasional convulsions as a goal was scored or in the wilder expressions of scorn and hatred for the other end, was there any feeling of danger. Indeed, on reflection the whole occasion, while garbed in some unattractive features, seemed to heighten that sense of family which the New Year either fosters or imposes upon you. You belonged to your group and in such a big crowd you felt quite invulnerable, protected and secure. It made winter and New Year bearable and was marred only when you heard that nature had played tricks on everyone by converting Glasgow to Arctic tundra, thus producing that most despised of all adult comments in those days: 'The gemme's aff.'

At the end of these Ne'erday games at Celtic Park or Ibrox we were swept off the terraces by a tide of humanity, our feet never touching the ground until we were in the street. It was like an exhilarating ride on a roller-coaster. It all seemed so innocent and harmless and safe. It wasn't, though.

In 1971 New Year's Day fell on a Friday, but in keeping with the attempts to control any possible trouble the game was to be played the day after. That day of respite, as had been intended all along, added an obvious and significant degree of sobriety to the occasion, for the 80 000 crowd was described later as one of the best behaved in the history of the series. The players were also commended for having played in a very sporting manner, which could only improve the notorious image of the fixture. But these views were uttered in retrospect by people with an acute awareness of their bitterly ironic ring, for within a very few minutes of that game ending sixty-six people lay dead on stairway 13 at the Copland Road end of Ibrox Park.

In the light of subsequent events it is very difficult to avoid looking for portents or accentuating the funereal greyness of the day. And yet, with an almost eerie sense of foreboding, the *Glasgow Herald* of that very morning had produced an editorial the main thrust of which was an expression of relief at having got 1970 behind us all. It described the old year as 'a year of disasters including earthquakes in Peru, death and destruction on a monumental scale in Pakistan, a terrible fire at a French dance hall and the loss of the Fraserburgh lifeboat'. No prophecy was contained, but in the reading of those words that morning one might have been forgiven for feeling immensely secure at engaging in nothing more vicarious in life than going to a football match.

Those still suffering residual hangovers on that Saturday would not have been helped by the weather, which was itself liverish. The city was thinly veiled by a chilling mist, which did not augur well for the match because the Govan district of Glasgow, beside the River Clyde, could well claim to have been the world's cradle of fogs. An overnight frost had set in throughout the country and hardened the grounds. Glasgow, still not aroused from its Ne'erday slumbers, seemed desolate outside the main routes to Ibrox, which were thronged by crowds split not only by colour but by disposition to this game, for a depleted Rangers had lost 3–1 at Falkirk the previous day and were well out of contention in the League, leaving their supporters to take a pessimistic view of the approaching match. Celtic, after all, were shaping well enough to win their sixth consecutive League title. Only Aberdeen, heading the League at that stage by three points with Celtic having a game in hand, were likely to stop them. But pessimism has never driven Old Firm supporters to dereliction of duty, and a massive Rangers support converged, albeit apprehensively, on the stadium.

2 January 1971	**Rangers 1 Celtic 1** (League match)	Ibrox Stadium

Rangers: Neef, Jardine, Mathieson, Greig, McKinnon, Jackson, Henderson (Mac-Donald), Conn, D. Johnstone, Smith, Stein

Celtic: Williams, Craig, Gemmell, Brogan, Connelly, Hay, J. Johnstone, Hood, Wallace, Callaghan, Lennox

Scorers: Stein (90); J. Johnstone (89)

Referee: W. Anderson (East Kilbride)   *att*: 80 000

In looking back at the contemporary reports of this match you sense the reluctance on anyone's part to recall this game in detail, almost as if to do so would be an act of irreverence. Words lie reluctantly on pages as if drained of the usual passion that the game normally evokes. There is almost a sense of guilt pervading them, as if the disaster ought to have eradicated all evidence that a sporting event had ever taken place.

From the outset it was clear that this huge crowd was to see football severely constrained by the concrete-like pitch. On such an unyielding surface movement was restricted, running at full pace was hazardous and mistakes multiplied as a result. But the game was open enough, with the contrast in styles very apparent: Celtic built their moves carefully and methodically, while Rangers relied mainly on long punts up field which, given the surface, was not a bad tactic. Jimmy Johnstone, capable of playing well on broken glass let alone a concrete pitch, was from the outset one of the few players to express himself properly. Alfie Conn of Rangers was another. Their skill glimmered sparingly. The game looked like ending in a draw even from early on. It did eventually, but in the most catastrophic way. In the 89th minute Celtic scored. Harry Hood, who played in midfield for Celtic that day, recalls the goal.

> I just remember the last two minutes of the game nothing else. Everything outside of that is just a blur. But our goal, when it came, I thought would end the day. Bobby Lennox hit a tremendous shot which came off the bar, and Jimmy Johnstone of all people, one of the smallest players on the park, headed the rebound into the net. I honestly thought that was it. I didn't know precisely how much time was left but I knew the final whistle would go soon. But I'll always recall what happened next. Rangers centred the ball quickly, and I can see the ball being thumped down their left wing and Jim Craig giving away a free kick. I'll remember that free kick for ever.'

It was taken by Dave Smith. He swung the ball across the penalty area. It bounced hazardously among the swinging boots, Johnstone poked a foot at it, but Colin Stein, following up, hammered the ball into the net. Within almost exactly sixty seconds Rangers had equalised. Fifteen seconds later the referee blew the final whistle.

Thousands of Rangers supporters who had started to leave the ground immediately Celtic had scored heard the roar from their own crowd as the equaliser went in. Hundreds on stairway 13 which led down to the exit and who were already at the foot of the steps suddenly turned back and surged upwards. They were met by the flood of people still pouring down. In this unnatural meeting of tides someone tripped and turned the mass of bodies into a vortex of disaster on an unprecedented scale. People suddenly toppled downwards. The momentum swelled into a tumult as the pressure increased into a tidal wave of falling bodies. In a few seconds they had piled on top of each other in a frantic writhing mass from which, for those underneath, there was no escape. The sheer density of crowd made it difficult for the surrounding and safer crowd to make any instant efforts at rescue. It took only those few seconds for people to die.

When the first goal had been scored every sports desk round the country had erupted almost like the crowd at Ibrox, for it looked like the sort of finish that would see many a writer preparing eulogies on another Jock Stein triumph. Now, they all had to claw back the sentiments and make sense of the stunning and unexpected equaliser. The BBC sports department was no exception. But amidst the flurry of activity and that routine state of late Saturday afternoon pandemonium, Frank Bough's avuncular tones were suddenly heard from the *Grandstand* studio as he said in a tone of incredulity, 'We hear that many people have been killed in an accident at Ibrox. Latest reports say twenty-two.' The office suddenly became very quiet, and my own Glasgow instinct surfaced immediately and erroneously as I thought that it must have been the result of a pitched battle.

The news filtering back was vague. The radio commentators had already departed leaving only one reporter to prepare an account of the game for BBC World Service, thus limiting the most valuable means of quick communication, especially as he sat in a corner of the press box as far away from the scene of the accident as it was possible to be. An entire BBC Television outside broadcast unit which had covered the game for late-evening transmission had packed up, calmly tucked away their equipment for the night, and driven back to their base at East Kilbride just outside the city and went home completely unaware of what had happened, despite the fact that every news programme within the BBC was screaming for some sort of coverage.

Detective Superintendent Joe Beattie, the man who had led the hunt for the notorious Glasgow murderer 'Bible John', and who had gone home from the game, like many others, completely in the dark about the incident, received a phone call from the Chief Constable of Glasgow, Sir James Robertson, asking him to return immediately to the stadium and take charge of the investigation. He would have arrived back at Ibrox at about the time we did in search of more information about an event the horrific statistics of which were beginning to sound incredible. Beattie went to examine the dead and the injured. They were still ferrying bodies across the ground from the original scene of carnage on the steps of stairway 13. He was accustomed to death; we were not.

It looked as if an earthquake had hit Ibrox, with its epicentre on that steep slope of steps which led out to Copland Road and the Glasgow Underground. Although we had set out with the well-intentioned aim of seeking more

The ambulance services were not slow in getting to Ibrox

information on what exactly had happened, suddenly we found that we could not cope as well as we had thought and that it was not the time for the unprofessional eye to be looking for causes, as even then Joe Beattie was doing, when it was difficult enough to suppress the feelings of nausea and incomprehension.

The bodies had been laid out on the hard track underneath the Ibrox stand. All the dead had blackened faces, as if in their struggle for life they had been touched by some macabre cosmetic. It did not require too much calculation by the police to determine that what they were seeing was clear evidence of a mass of people who had fought desperately but unsuccessfully for air to breathe. They took the injured into both dressing-rooms where the players had to make a quick evacuation. Sandy Jardine, the Rangers full-back, remembers the horrifying scene.

> We were in the bath enjoying ourselves after getting that late equaliser when Jock Wallace came in and shouted for us to get out, there was an emergency. But even before we could start drying ourselves they were bringing in the injured. In just a few minutes the floor was covered with people lying there moaning. It was incredible. You would have thought there had been a war outside. Then we heard about the dead. We just went home, numb.'

RANGERS
V
CELTIC
80

John Burrowes, then news editor of the *Daily Record*, which was on strike, had gone to Ibrox to piece together the whole tragic story so that with two other colleagues he could produce a report for that week's edition of the *Sunday Mail*. He had just returned from Vietnam after a tour of duty but even he, who believed himself hardened by the daily witness of the awfulness of war and the frequent sight of napalmed bodies, was peculiarly affected when afterwards in a hospital he saw one man bending over his dead friend, saying over and over again, 'Jimmy, I promise as long as I live we will never go to an Old Firm match again. Jimmy, I promise. I promise.'

In his first survey of stairway 13 Joe Beattie could see that an immense force had buckled the central steel barriers which ran up the steps vertically like thin spines. Some of them had been twisted in such a manner that they looked about as formidable a buttress as burnt-out matchsticks. The outer barriers which formed the perimeter of the stairway had held solid. They were firmly grounded railway sleepers. Beattie knew, too, that although they were dealing with an accident of a quite unprecedented nature, this stairway had not been without danger and that three serious accidents had occurred there previously, with two fatalities as a result of crushing. He realised he would have to bring this matter up right away with the board of directors.

The ambulances were shuttling the bodies to the city mortuary and they had even considered using a school gym or Milne's Cold Store near Glassford Street. As they did so we returned to the studios, and my own feeling was that putting out a programme at all that night would be tasteless. But we realised there would be logistical difficulties involved in having no sport at all at that time of the evening with nothing comparable to replace it. We sat around for a while in silence, nobody wishing to risk uttering the first practical idea on a night when you instinctively felt the entire nation should be quietly shutting down. But this editorial meeting gradually developed into a discussion on

Grim and shocked Jock
Wallace pitched himself
into helping survivors

broadcasting ethics. Two of us had suggested that it would be the height of
bad taste to show highlights of the game if we were obliged to produce a
programme at all. We stuck to that position although we realised it was bound
to cause problems of replacement. The discussion sharpened. Suddenly a senior
executive in a fit of professional detachment developed a new and breathtaking
approach. 'How many were killed remind me?' he asked. I told him. 'Sixty-
six.' I recall him sitting back in perfect relaxation. 'How many were at the
game?' he went on. Again I replied wondering where this line of questioning
was taking us. 'The attendance was 80 000.' He paused for a moment and
without the slightest flicker of emotion he replied, 'Sixty-six out of 80 000. It's
not all that many, is it?' I recall the silence that followed which I could only
assume was akin to the terrifying moments during the war when people heard
the buzz-bombs until the last few moments and then waited with bated breath
for the impact. The statistical evaluation was like doing a sum on the back of
a coffin. I ventured an opinion barely able to conceal my anger. 'I suppose if
this were a mining or fireman's disaster and not just some football supporters
you wouldn't be thinking like that.' It was barely adequate but all I could
summon up under the circumstances. The dialogue drew a disapproving and
magisterial 'Tut-tut' from the man who was going to make the final decision
on the matter. Diplomatically he moved on to distance us from the original
remark which had even shaken him.

But we were discovering that tragedy evokes a gravity of mood that can
easily distort the thinking of those who have to try to make some sense of it.
We seemed weighed down by a haunting humourlessness. Men who had
professional regard for one another snarled at each other like a family squab-
bling over an heirloom. Eventually, we decided to put out a programme
covering only English football and pushed the Rangers–Celtic game on to a

shelf in the BBC library, where it has lain unopened to this day.

Detective Superintendent Joe Beattie and his officers saw to the grooming of the bodies. He ensured they had their faces washed, their ties (if they remained) straightened, their tattered clothing made to look more presentable, and their hair combed. Five boys from one small village in Markinch had died. An eighteen-year-old girl who had made a doll as a Christmas present for the baby daughter of Colin Stein the man who had scored Rangers' equaliser, lay dead. Young and old alike, friends, fathers, sons, neighbours – the list of dead seemed cruelly representative, as if fate had wanted on that day a perfect cross-section of an ordinary crowd as the victims. Officially, they had suffered 'traumatic asphyxiation'. They had not been able to breathe.

Beattie then went to the Ibrox boardroom. The scene there was one of disarray. Expecting to launch into his first dialogue on the scenes of carnage he was taken aback to be greeted by a Rangers director David Hope as a long lost friend. They had played junior football together in their youth and suddenly before anything else could be mentioned Hope launched into reminiscences of their playing days at Ashfield Junior Football Club. Beattie could be very blunt and direct when required but preferred on this occasion despite suffering intense frustration at the irrelevance of this to let the unexpected reminiscing simply peter out perhaps realising that men in shock might let their minds wander off at tangents as a convenient refuge. But it gave Beattie the initial impression that the Ibrox board simply had not grasped the enormity of the situation. The directors' recollection of previous accidents and the consequent visit of Chief Superintendent Nicholson to inspect the stairway some months earlier was disturbingly vague. Nobody could remember who had accompanied the police on their inspection and, indeed, Joe Beattie gained the impression that some immediate buck-passing was going on. There seemed

The funeral of the
McLean brothers from
Slamannan near Falkirk.
Victims of the disaster

The Old Firm managers
united in grief after a
memorial service

Glasgow Cathedral
packed with Protestant
and Catholic mourners at
a memorial service

to be an initial fear of some blame being apportioned in their direction. In his view this state of disarray would have persisted to the point of disintegration had Rangers at that critical point in their history not possessed the strong personality of Willie Waddell.

Without Waddell the club might have have seemed enormously vulnerable, because none of the directors seemed to know how to express himself other than with the customary feelings of regret. Waddell mastered the situation immediately. As the rest of the board of directors gave no clear indication of having sufficient intellectual stature to comprehend the enormous implications involved, Waddell towered over the others in instantly grasping the dimension

of the task facing Rangers in rehabilitating themselves from this enormous psychological blow. He clearly realised that it was not just Ibrox Stadium that would be under scrutiny but Rangers Football Club itself, in the manner in which it showed care and concern and openness about any detail of the disaster. For Willie Waddell it assumed the importance of a personal crusade. Sandy Jardine recalls:

> The manager was brilliant. He did everything. I don't think he slept for months. He couldn't have, with the amount of work he put in. We were all organised to go to the various funerals and to visit the injured in hospital. No training was done. The whole experience drained us. Then, when we played our first game back at Ibrox weeks after, it was like being in a trance. The atmosphere was just unreal, very down and quiet. It took a long, long time to recover.'

The official inquiry criticised the club for certain aspects of the way they conducted their business in relation to safety at the stadium. But they were exonerated from principal blame for the specific accident that occurred that day on Stairway 13. It would therefore be convenient to perceive this as purely Rangers' disaster. But the responsibilities have to be much more widely shared than that. Indeed it could be said that many of us were culpable. There were those of us who had neither written nor spoken a single word previously about the conditions for spectators around the country. And after all Ibrox was considered much safer than most. There were those football directors up and down the country and who might have been clones of some of the Ibrox board who joined clubs purely for prestigious reasons and gave little consideration to the consumers' interests. They were good at counting heads but gave little consideration to the rest of the anatomy. There were the punters themselves who would have far rather clubs spent money on players than invest in more seats or toilets. Thus the herding instinct, leading directly to a massive health risk, was mutually approved by both boardroom and terracing. It was within the crude cosiness of football's general conventions that the Ibrox disaster occurred. The accident was freakish, the conditions appallingly normal.

Yet we know now, that with their modern stadium born of the ideas of Willie Waddell and which is the envy of many in Europe, Rangers have created a model for others to follow. We also know rather more painfully that despite Lord Wheatley's Commission on Ground Safety which was set up immediately afterwards that change in football seems too often to be at the pace at which it took paleolithic man to become an urban commuter. We know that the almost primitive hunger to see this sport and to support a favourite team is not only frequently underestimated but can easily obliterate the lessons of the past. This is the only conclusion one can reach when you trace the path from that winter's day in Glasgow in 1971 to the tragic spring afternoon at Hillsborough Sheffield eighteen years later.

CHAPTER NINE

THE CENTENARY STUDS

When Jock Wallace came to Ibrox in December 1969 he brought with him the reputation of a man who had spent much of his life proving that Darwin had wasted his time travelling to the Galapagos Islands to discover that only the fittest of the species survive. He had only needed to travel a few hundred yards or so to work in the coal mines of East Lothian to conclude that if you weren't physically fit, you sank. Fixing bayonets against the Communist insurrection in Malaysia in his twenties merely confirmed his youthful beliefs. As a goalkeeper he showed muscle and bravery and is to this day credited with plotting Rangers' famous downfall in the Scottish Cup in 1967 when, as Berwick Rangers' player-manager, he saw his side make a considerable historical dent in the Glasgow team's image by knocking them out 1–0. Wallace enjoyed that legend, although objective witnesses to that spectacle would have said that Rangers were so appallingly inept that the Glenbuck Cherrypickers might have stood a chance against them that day. What was undisputed was Wallace's zealous devotion to physical fitness, which bordered almost on mania. It is not that he disliked weaklings, rather that he made you feel they were of an alien species that would just wither away naturally.

Willie Waddell plucked him from Hearts because the new Rangers manager had seen his old club take on an almost effete quality since the days he had been there as a player, and felt that concrete had to be poured into its foundations to form a solid base. Wallace was to be the steel-bender. The formula worked outstandingly well on the afternoon of 5 May 1973, on the occasion of the Centenary Scottish Cup Final.

I once interviewed Wallace on the television platform at Pittodrie and asked him what he had thought of the opposition, Aberdeen. He looked at me with a mixture of disbelief and contempt as if I had asked how much he approved the tactics of the Communist guerrillas in Malaysia. 'I only watch one team, the Rangers,' was his blunt riposte. Of course, he knew perfectly well how well Aberdeen could and did play that day, but it seemed consistent with the image to present this bluff, totally committed side of himself to the world – an absolute believer in Rangers being the centre of the universe. He also knew where this would be popular: the terraces. They loved him for it, and most still did even when he fell on hard times at Ibrox.

Soon after he arrived as coach he embarked on a fitness programme which looked at first as if he had borrowed ideas from Lord Lovat's wartime commandos. The players were taken to the other side of the country and introduced to the sand dunes of Gullane, a part of the world Wallace knew

The only buckets on this shore were those containing the sweat of the Rangers' players on Gullane's 'Murder Hill'

well from his childhood. The dunes there might well be confused with the foothills of the Himalayas. If the Rangers players were thought not to like this, certainly the comedians, cartoonists and the media in general did.

The regime was lampooned mercilessly. And yet there was nothing unique in this as other clubs had used dune training before, and some outward-bound techniques in pre-season preparations were not unknown, such as when Celtic had used the slopes of Ben Lomond a couple of decades earlier. But then the arrival of Waddell at Ibrox had created such an air of expectancy around the country, and his appointment of a well-known fitness fanatic meant that a venture like this could not go without comment. Yet there were some who, although they admitted it was a not uncommon occurrence to see what appeared to be a fully fit footballer crouching on the sand vomiting, actually enjoyed the experience. Tom Forsyth, who was to score one of the most bizarre winning goals of any Cup Final, had few complaints about the dunes, one of which was dubbed 'Murder Hill'.

> Really the players used to enjoy going away out of the stadium and Glasgow to the east coast. It added variety to training, which could become very boring. It was hard, yes, and some of them used to be sick after some of the tough runs. But nobody complained, and I don't mean because they were scared to because of Big Jock. And anyway we were all benefiting from it, because we were chasing Celtic hard and determined to catch them.'

'Chasing Celtic' would, on reflection, seem a mild way of describing the respective positions of both clubs in the early part of the season 1972–3. In the first League game, played at Hampden Park because of ground renovation at Parkhead, and with a midday kick-off as part of a move to counter possible crowd trouble, Rangers had been humiliated – as indicated at the tail end of the game when, with hardly a Rangers supporter left in Hampden, John Greig scored at the Celtic end and for the first time in living memory raised a cheer from the green and white masses. It sounded bitterly ironic, however; Old Firm supporters are particularly skilled in adding insult to injury. The greatly heralded Rangers resurgence, much anticipated after winning the Cup Winners' Cup in Barcelona against Moscow Dynamo in May 1972, seemed to be fizzling out.

In truth, the club had suffered a terrible mauling in the aftermath of the crowd riots and battles with the police after the game in Barcelona, and although at the time they put a brave face on it, the ultimate banning from Europe traumatised them. Willie Waddell became involved in an almost personal crusade, both to reduce the two-year ban to one (which he did) and more importantly to remove the stain on the club's name. The turmoil that all of this generated diverted Waddell's creative energies away from the playing side of the club just when the momentum of their European success needed consolidating. Equally debilitating was the great sense of let-down in that their justifiable triumph clashed with the opprobrium provoked around Europe. It seemed to envelop the club in gloom for a long time, and players appeared to lose their hunger for the game, as Rangers winger Willie Johnston reflected later when he wrote: 'Ibrox seemed to be in a trough of anti-climax after Barcelona. The manager seemed to be of the opinion that some of the players

Jock Wallace and Jock Stein

who had won the Cup Winners' Cup had nothing more to prove.'

The early season results seemed to bear that out and when it looked as if Celtic, rubbing in their win at the temporary home at Hampden, would streak away from them, Jock Wallace went into the transfer market and bought a player who in retrospect might be said to have been the most significant buy he ever made in his life, Tom Forsyth.

If Jock Wallace were to want to come back to this life as anyone else, I suspect it would be as Tom Forsyth. The big central defender, then playing for Motherwell, possessed everything that Wallace espoused in the game. He had, in a phrase beloved by Wallace and used by him in virtually every television interview I ever made with him, 'character and determination'. Wallace saw in him a man prepared to demolish a brick wall or deliver opponents tackles they would never forget. He had a running lope which always seemed too long for his height but which intimated an awesome conviction when he picked up pace. Forsyth, it could be said, stemmed the blood flowing from the club at that time, for from the moment of his arrival at Ibrox until the end of the season Rangers never lost a game.

Some people did not take kindly to Forsyth and, indeed, the man is still stung by the recollection of Tommy Docherty suggesting that it would be appropriate for the Ranger to wear a 'butcher's apron'. To this day Forsyth in defending himself refers to 'the tackle'. Not any old tackle, of which he had many, but that special one that seemed the answer to all his critics which occurred in the game against England at Hampden in 1976 when, running behind Mick Channon in the penalty area, he contrived to reach out a long leg and whip the ball away just as the Englishman was about to score. That he did not touch flesh, that he did not concede a penalty but saved the day for Scotland brought the house down. But he was an exceptionally hard player and for that reason people were either blinded to his other qualities or very reluctant to accept that he was more than just a kicker. For instance, when he toured with the Scottish team in Argentina and Brazil in 1977 he was, according to some of us in the party, quite magnificent as a sweeper without once incurring the wrath of the touchy South American referees. Yet the media gave their 'Player of the Tour' award to the ever lovable Alan Rough. It was safe to do so. Forsyth by then had amassed a reputation which meant that some people felt that to give him an award for football would be like granting parole to a perpetual offender.

Jock Stein was never one to concede too much to Rangers in public, but in private he was impressed by the way they had seemed to sort themselves out since their early season débâcle and had dug in tenaciously, putting an unexpected strain on Celtic. But it wasn't enough. The Saturday before the Centenary Cup Final Celtic had achieved their eighth consecutive League Championship and in doing so made themselves hot favourites for the Final, because their opponents, for all that they had had a run of twenty-five games in a row unbeaten, had nothing to show for it in this, their own centenary year.

Saturday 5 May was a wet one, but it did not diminish the appetite for the game and a huge crowd showed up under leaden skies. For the first time royalty graced a Scottish Cup Final, in the person of Princess Alexandra. This

5 May 1973	**Rangers 3 Celtic 2** (Scottish Cup Final)	Hampden Park

Rangers: McCloy, Jardine, Mathieson, Greig, D. Johnstone, MacDonald, McLean, Forsyth, Parlane, Conn, Young

Celtic: Hunter, McGrain, Brogan (Lennox), Murdoch, McNeill, Connelly, J. Johnstone, Deans, Dalglish, Hay, Callaghan

Scorers: (Parlane (35), Conn (46), Forsyth (60); Dalglish (25), Connelly (52, pen.)

Referee: J.R.P. Gordon (Newport-on-Tay)   att: 122 714

official acknowledgement of the game was all the more welcome to hard-pressed football officials who were worried about the image of a game increasingly tarnished by football hooliganism throughout Britain. Sociologists and anthropologists were beginning to see football as a fertile area for examination, and one of the most popular of these, Desmond Morris, wrote at the time that a football club was 'organised like a small tribe complete with a tribal territory, tribal elders, witch doctors, heroes, camp followers and other assorted tribesmen'. A sweeping glance around Hampden that day might have confirmed all his theories. Whether as tribesman or hero, Kenny Dalglish put on his Celtic jersey typically unperturbed by either the atmosphere outside or the intense pre-match build-up.

■ People used to ask me how I felt playing against a team I had supported as a boy. Nothing. That's how I felt. I had never let the Rangers and Celtic aggro ever affect me, even when I was a boy. I was a professional player playing for a club with a big support and that was what went through my head. I remember the first time I played against them. It was at Ibrox and we were awarded a penalty. I didn't expect to be taking it considering it was my Old Firm début, but Billy McNeill came up to me and asked me to take the kick. I was a bit surprised but it didn't bother me too much. Just when I was about to run up I noticed my lace had come undone so I bent down and carefully and slowly tied it back in place. I know a lot of people must have thought I was suffering a great strain. But I wasn't. I just stood up and scored. I took these games in my stride, which is why I thought we had the beating of Rangers that day before the game, and certainly after I had scored the opening goal. We always beat Rangers for pace up front and so we liked to draw them up field a bit, then hit them with quick balls. That's what happened when Dixie Deans slipped the ball past two defenders and allowed me to run on to the through ball. I saw Peter McCloy coming out of his goal but I just kept my head down and swept it past him. It wasn't a bad start.'

Just, in fact, the kind of start most people had expected. After twenty-five minutes Celtic, the favourites, had gone in front and there was nothing to indicate that anything might alter the trend. It is here that the motivational powers of Jock Wallace might well have influenced Rangers' ability to take that one on the chin and bounce back – which they did, as Tom Forsyth describes.

■ Jock could fire you up. He had a particular way of getting Alec MacDonald

needled before a game so that the wee man would get really involved. He did that day as well. There wasn't a man went out on the park who didn't know how important the game was to the club. That's why it didn't surprise me when Alec made the equaliser. I saw him picking up the ball on the left wing and making a run. It was a great ball to the near post and Derek Parlane seemed to take it right on the forehead and send it down almost straight through Hunter. You just can't believe the way we felt after that. Not just back in it again, but taking the game right to them.'

Too many cooks spoiling the broth. Seven Celtic defenders yet Derek Parlane scores the equaliser for Rangers

Jim Brogan steeplechases behind the ball but cannot prevent Alfie Conn scoring Rangers' second

Immediately after the interval and with the score 1–1, Rangers took the lead in a most significant fashion. It was the sort of goal that one had become accustomed to watching Celtic score, a goal based on a player fleet of foot leaving a defender stranded. This time it was the youthful Alfie Conn showing Billy McNeill a clean pair of heels and slipping the ball past the advancing Hunter. Given the current circumstances in football in Scotland, there was a feeling of incredulity among the watching media representatives in particular at the fact that Rangers had given Celtic a goal start and yet within a minute of the beginning of the second half were now in the lead 2–1. It seemed much more logical for Celtic to fight back and equalise – which they did. Six minutes later John Greig, standing on his goal-line, had little alternative but to punch out a shot by Deans which was heading for the net. George Connelly stepped up to take the penalty. Kenny Dalglish recalls:

6   Nobody could do it better. People keep saying to me what a tragedy George Connelly was in the game; what a wasted talent. I don't understand that. He was a great player and I remember all the tricks he could do with the ball. But he made his own decisions about life. If he didn't want to go on and become one of the greatest ever Celtic players, then that was up to him. Why does everybody feel so sorry for him? He was unreliable, I know that, and he could suddenly disappear and not even the manager would know where he was, but when he was on his game he was great and that day I had no doubts about him taking the kick.'

Connelly sent McCloy the wrong way, and Celtic were level. Expectations were probably now on a Celtic win. Stein, after all, had firmly established his reputation of pulling a fast one time and time again over his old rivals. We waited for the *coup de grâce*, but it never came. At least, not from the source we anticipated. Eight minutes later Hampden was graced by a goal which will be remembered by all those who feel that a touch of the bizarre is never entirely unwelcome in a Cup Final. Tommy McLean, the diminutive Rangers winger who, realising that Hunter, the Celtic goalkeeper, was making his début in an Old Firm game, had been tormenting him with his finely judged crosses into goal, prepared to take a free kick.

6   Most times I took a free kick I looked up to see where Derek Johnstone would be. I always wanted to give him enough time to run in towards the cross, so I usually aimed for a few yards in front of him, and, since we had a good understanding about that, we did quite well out of these situations. This time I did exactly that and I saw him rushing in and getting his head to it. I didn't know at the time where Big Tam was.'

Tom Forsyth was close to Johnstone.

Derek Parlane unleashes power, Billy McNeill unleashes a withering look

> I saw the ball coming off Johnstone's head and to my horror the ball rolled along the line and hit the other post. Now I don't know how I came to be standing on their goal-line, let alone being unmarked in the first place. Nobody had told me to go there. It wasn't part of any tactic. I just went. And there it was in front of me, the ball moving slowly back along the line. I can remember just sticking out my leg and sort of missing it. I actually caught it with the studs and didn't give it enough movement, then I got some weight behind it and pushed it over the line from just a few inches. Then I just went berserk. I remember running up the field waving my arms. I wasn't used to this because I'd never scored a goal for the club before that. All right, it wasn't the greatest goal that's ever been scored, but it's the only one I'll never forget.'

There was no fight back by Celtic after that. Both MacDonald and Conn, in fact, could have added to Rangers' score as their command of the game became more evident. To be beaten by a goal scored from six inches and from the inaccurately-aimed studs of a boot is not a memory Jock Stein will have relished from that day. More serious for the future were the lessons to be drawn from Rangers' attack, which had shown Billy McNeill to be short on pace and the Celtic defence (as witness the winning goal) lacking in co-ordination. Stein was always a quick learner.

After the Cup presentation I interviewed Jock Wallace, seated in the enclosure. He looked composed but drained, his face pale and pinched. The interview, which went out live on *Grandstand*, was like talking to a man in a trance; he kept looking over my shoulder as if seeking peace somewhere on the horizon.

Alec MacDonald's fine leap came to nothing

Unknown to me he was in fact keeping his eye on general manager Willie Waddell, who had come to the track to find him for his presentation to Princess Alexandra. Waddell was in a towering rage on the track, and Jock knew it. At that stage of their partnership Wallace owed a great deal to the acumen and insight of Waddell and was generally compliant. I have to say, though, that they did not look like a couple who had just won the SFA Centenary Cup Final in their own centenary year against their old rivals.

The massive crowd went homewards in the rain, having behaved themselves generally well. In their midst, standing on the terraces, had been one of Britain's leading experts on football hooliganism, sociologist Ian Taylor from Sheffield University, who had been asked by the *Daily Record* to analyse the behaviour of this unique crowd. He summarised it as follows.

> If there is any religious significance bound up in Rangers and Celtic then I would describe it this way. It has nothing to do with Catholicism and Presbyterianism, because by far the majority on the terracings are not church-goers. From a sociologist's point of view Celtic and Rangers don't divide a city, they unite it, giving it a great soul. If there was no football the fans would rebel about the composition of the Corporation, the Welfare Department or similar services. It's not a religious fight. It's a social one.'

We could have saved him the money and effort in reaching that conclusion. As a sociologist perhaps he would have not taken too kindly to Jock Wallace's exhortation to his players before the game. 'It's fixed-bayonets time!' he had told them. The players, as well as the supporters, knew what he meant. Perhaps Charles Darwin would have understood as well.

The goal that won the cup. Tom Forsyth deliberates on whether to score or miss

CHAPTER TEN

THE LAST HURRAH

In the early summer of 1975 it was difficult to absorb the fact that Jock Stein was lying unconscious in the ward of a hospital in Dumfries, fighting for his life after a car accident. His immense stature did not seem to countenance accidents. He had always looked invulnerable to anything other than the apparently irresistible entreaties of the *Sporting Life* and unco-operative racehorses. I was in Italy at the time, and the sporting press without exception had made the horrendous car smash front-page news. The Italians had not forgotten what Stein had got up to in Lisbon in 1967 when Inter Milan had come home humiliated. They had developed lasting respect for the man who had taught them a lesson.

It was eight years on from that European Cup triumph in Portugal, and Stein had changed. He had carried an enormous burden over that period and seemed reluctant to change his exhausting commitment to the job which still kept him central to virtually all the major decisions taken at Celtic Park. Certainly he did not like to delegate and was never overkeen to accept advice, even from his closest colleagues. His prodigious work rate was legendary and he was still prepared to live up to it even though in January 1973 he had been taken to hospital with a suspected heart attack. But there were indications that he was tiring. He had made some signings which puzzled supporters and perplexed those who thought he had an unfailing touch when it came to selecting players for Celtic Park.

Even his tongue, which could effectively and gleefully shoot down journalists from time to time like a big-game hunter on perpetual safari, had softened. In April 1975, two days after I had described Colin Stein's championship-clinching goal for Rangers against Hibs at Easter Road on television, he saw me at a function and his irreverent smile put me on my guard. But all he said was, 'When Colin Stein scored I thought you were going to come right through the television screen.' Compared with the Stein of the past, this was like a judge letting off a drunk driver with a pardon.

On a Saturday morning in July 1975, coming back from holiday and driving the Mercedes car which belonged to his bookmaker friend Tony Queen who was a fellow passenger, he drove at speed head-on into another car coming down the wrong side of the dual carriageway just outside Lockerbie in the south of Scotland. It was a terrible smash, and something of a miracle that nobody died outright. Even in the immediate aftermath of the jumbled mess of cars and bodies Stein was conscious enough to appreciate the droll aspect of a young constable leaning over him. He told me, 'I couldn't breathe. I was struggling. And there was this young face bending over me that kept on

... from which he survived. The crashed Mercedes outside Lockerbie

asking, "Could you blow into this, please?" I couldn't even tell him what to do with his bag.'

Being able himself to appreciate the absurd situation of one of Scotland's most famous teetotallers lying among the wreckage and being asked to take a breathalyser seemed to give him that very tiny grip on life which he desperately needed there and then, and which through his strength of character he refused to relinquish. But Stein on a life-support machine and during his period of recuperation was like a man in captivity, for he had always been the most restless of men. He had to suffer the agonies of absence from Celtic Park for nine months at a time when the club badly needed his expertise.

Sean Fallon, given the almost impossible task of reviving Celtic while Stein recovered, could not cope with the bristling resurgence of Rangers, who won the treble under the management of Jock Wallace in season 1975–6. Deprived of Stein's leadership, Celtic Football Club had taken on the pallor of mediocrity.

That he was not the same man when he returned to Parkhead officially was scarcely surprising. Anyone a breath away from death, and perhaps feeling, although without foundation, some responsibility for the accident having been at the wheel, could hardly make a total recovery. He had signed Andy Lynch from Hearts. Andy, a clean-cut player of pace who had been a winger, then converted to full-back, was among the group of players aware of the change that had taken place in the man.

6 When he first came back he was jumpier and more nervy than I'd ever seen him and much less tolerant of people, which I suppose was to be expected. Now we were really struggling. Frankly, we lacked some class players, and equally frankly I think Jock had made some mistakes in some of his signings prior to his accident, so he maybe had an even harder job to face up to than

Celtic fans at Hampden Park

when he first came to Parkhead, because then he had a lot of young players who were just beginning to break through at the right time for him. Now he was facing a massive rebuilding and, to be honest, with Rangers doing so well I began to doubt if he could do it. But, of course, it was then he began to show his old shrewdness. One of the best things he did was to buy Pat Stanton in a part exchange for Jackie McNamara. Stanton was class. He had style and read the game well, and playing tucked in behind our big defenders you might have thought Big Jock had him specially created just for the job. That gave us stability. We became more and more confident and so did the Big Man. You could see his whole personality returning to something like his old self. We began to get results, and in beating Rangers twice in the League that season it must have seemed like old times to him.'

Not quite. Celtic had won the League Championship in his first season back, but he wanted more. He wanted to win the double in a straight head-on clash with Jock Wallace. Saturday 7 May of that year gave him the opportunity.

| 7 May 1977 | **Celtic 1   Rangers 0**
(Scottish Cup Final) | Hampden Park |

Celtic: Latchford, McGrain, Lynch, Stanton, R. MacDonald, Aitken, Dalglish, Edvaldsson, Craig, Wilson, Conn

Rangers: Kennedy, Jardine, Greig, Forsyth, Jackson, Watson (Robertson), McLean, Hamilton, Parlane, A. MacDonald, Johnstone

Scorer: Lynch (20, pen.)

Referee: R.B. Valentine (Dundee)   *att*: 54 252

Times were not good for football. There was a marked decline in attendances around the country, not helped of course by the previous season's showing by Celtic. The Celtic chairman, Desmond White, maintaining the view first aired by his predecessor Sir Robert Kelly, continued to be the most articulate opponent of any extension of television coverage, regarding it as an insidious enemy of the game. He was probably the least impressed in the land at the news that the Scottish Cup Final this time would be covered live on the box. There was nothing the finalists could do about this for the SFA had arrived at a perfectly legitimate deal with their new sponsors Scottish and Newcastle Breweries who, in investing £250 000 for a three-year period, insisted on live television coverage. Those opponents of the deal luridly described it as a sell-out and warned of the demise of the game in the not-too-distant future. Whatever the prognostications, Scottish football was being introduced to the notion that the badly needed injection of sponsorship had inevitably to be wedded to extensive television coverage. So it has been ever since.

On the day of the Final it rained with a meanness that might have been wished upon the event by those who had predicted a calamitous effect on attendance by the live coverage. When the television production crew arrived at Hampden that morning there was not one who did not feel as if they were on trial in some way as they prepared for the first live Final in twenty years. Being this time in colour they were conscious of all elements concerning the perimeter of the pitch and the advertising boards, which on examination showed very little evidence of the sponsors who, for all the money they had sunk into the Final and their insistence on live television, were so low-profile as to be almost invisible.

Both managers played it almost exactly that way at the start and would not announce their teams until half an hour before kick-off, so that we went through the ritual-cum-charade of being told repeatedly in that last hour, 'I am not giving you my team until he gives you his.' When the announcements finally came it was Celtic's selection that caused the bigger surprise. Ronnie Glavin was out through injury. Johnny Doyle had been dropped in preference to Paul Wilson, and most interestingly of all Stein had introduced the Icelander Johannes Edvaldsson, who had never been on a winning side in the Glasgow derby.

As the cameras panned round the ground, the viewers at home were seeing Hampden at its bleakest. The wind and rain were forcing the spectators at the open Celtic end to use their flags and banners as protection against the elements. The SFA had announced they had sold 70 000 tickets, but in fact the official attendance was less than 55 000. Sitting at home watching was Willie Ormond, who only that week had resigned his job as manager of Scotland to take on the Hearts post. As the SFA had not included him in the official party that day, he had declined the offer of two ordinary stand tickets and stayed away. The stadium looked disturbingly unfilled, as if these two great clubs had suddenly fallen out of fashion. Instead of a colourful and crowded pageant, the viewers huddled in comfort inside were seeing something of a wet rag. The game, except for its one highly dramatic and controversial moment, sadly blended with the dreariness of the surrounds. Andy Lynch picks out the most significant feature for Celtic.

🄑 Playing Johannes Edvaldsson worked like a dream. He was told to mark Derek Johnstone; Roddy MacDonald was to look after Derek Parlane, and Pat Stanton was left to sweep up at the back. It couldn't have been better arranged because Derek Johnstone didn't get a kick or, more importantly, a header at the ball. Now Jock Wallace was a great big guy, a lovely human being; I had been coached by him when he had been at Tynecastle with Hearts. But frankly, his tactics against us were naive. All they were doing was punting high balls into the penalty area whenever they had possession, and that was right up our street. We perhaps had concentrated a bit more on defence, but Joe Craig up front was more dangerous than the two Rangers strikers put together and Kenny Dalglish, while I don't think he had one of his great games, always bothered them.'

Colin Jackson was at the centre of Rangers' defence.

🄑 Frankly, Jock Wallace was no match for Stein in terms of tactics, and apart from that all the Rangers players actually admired Stein. He was a players' man. I lived quite near him and got to know him as well as any Rangers player and he always seemed genuine in everything he did or said. To be honest, I wasn't the only Rangers player who wished we had been blessed by his tactical genius. Looking back we did hardly anything of any originality in that game, which I remember not just for the controversy but for being so bloody awful.'

With the Rangers attack being held comfortably, but Celtic not touching the heights, the game stuttered in its early stage rather than came alive, producing nothing more memorable than the sight of Alfie Conn who had meta-morphosed from blue, when four years earlier he had gained a winner's medal for Rangers in the Centenary Final, to green and white. Alfie was too laid back a character to be bothered by the hostility directed towards him by the Rangers supporters. But in the twentieth minute came chaos.

Conn took a corner which was headed on by MacDonald to Edvaldsson, who scooped it towards the line. What then happened is still a matter of furious debate among the players who were there, with views divided sharply according to which jersey they wore. From our position low down in the south-east enclosure it looked as if Derek Johnstone bent to stop the ball and it hit him somewhere either on the thigh or the hand since both were close together. The referee, Bob Valentine, pointed immediately to the penalty spot. He was chased around the box by the entire Rangers team who, having been angered by some of his decisions in the game at Pittodrie the previous week, and who had engaged in constant niggles with him during this game, suddenly boiled over. They were adamant that Johnstone had not handled the ball. Colin Jackson, Rangers' centre-half, was standing on the line and turned quickly to his right to see Johnstone standing beside the right-hand post. He is convinced the referee made a mistake.

🄑 Johnstone certainly had his hand beside his thigh, but the referee could not possibly have been clear in his mind that it had come off Derek's hand. The ball bounced straight back into play. If it had hit the hand it would have dropped straight down on the line. It didn't do that. I know it's now all dead and gone and we didn't deserve much out of that game, but I still think the referee blundered.'

The penalty incident. Did the ball hit accidentally or was the hand guilty of complicity?

The Celtic players were equally convinced he had not. Andy Lynch says he had a perfect view of it.

It hit his hand. There's no doubt in my mind about that. Anyway, all hell broke out as the Rangers players battled to try and change the mind of the referee. But, of course, it was no use. As all this was happening Kenny Dalglish picked up the ball and walked casually towards me with it. Now afterwards I read in the press that Kenny had decided not to take it and was looking for a volunteer. That's not the case. With Ronnie Glavin, our normal penalty-kick taker, not being able to play we had held a penalty-kick competition at Seamill the day before the Final and I won it. So it was decided that I should take the kicks. I told the boss I didn't want to and we had a right argument about it with Kenny, who wasn't too keen either. Suddenly Jock said to us, 'I wish it was me that got the chance to take a penalty for Celtic. Think yourselves lucky.' That did it. All doubts were removed. I was to take any penalty. What I didn't say to anybody was that I had only ever taken two penalty kicks in my life, both for Hearts, and I missed with both of them. Anyway, at that moment the ball seemed to disappear in the mêlée of players arguing with the referee. So I stood about twenty yards outside the box waiting my turn. When it began to calm down I walked forward and noticed that Stewart Kennedy, the Rangers goalkeeper, had the ball in his hands and was holding on to it as if somehow he was clinging to a last hope that the referee would change his mind. Then it became clear that he wouldn't. He suddenly looked at me and rolled the ball towards me, almost as if he had given up. I knew there and then I was going to score, and I did. I made up my mind to aim for his left-hand side and he never got near my shot. You know, it's virtually the only thing that people remember about me at Parkhead, despite everything else I did for the club.'

That is not too surprising, for that single kick won the Final. We replayed the incident which had produced the penalty over and over again without actually corroborating or negating the referee's decision. The action had been so quick

Referee Bob Valentine going suitably deaf in the face of Rangers' wrath. The penalty decision stood

Kenny Dalglish in his element. John Greig and Alec MacDonald in his wake and the camera at such distance from the incident that it was impossible to make a final judgement. Indeed, the game had been so drab that almost the only thing that viewers around the world eventually saw of the match was the re-run penalty incident, which produced lasting controversy. This, I must say, was to the delight of a rival brewer, who had a board right behind that particular goal and thus their product was displayed almost *ad nauseam* for a pittance compared with the money the sponsor had paid.

A drab Final simply accentuated the need to discuss the controversial penalty and the depressingly low attendance, for which live television coverage largely took the blame. There can be little doubt that the novelty of a televised game, compounded by the foul weather, kept people at home who would normally have attended. But despite a hostile press the SFA stood their ground, believing, as has since been proved justified, that while football had to be extremely vigilant about the use of television, live coverage of a special occasion such as the Scottish Cup Final need not hasten the decline of the game.

As the final whistle went, leaving Celtic winners by one goal to nothing, Jock Stein left his dug-out and shook the hands of his players as they left the field. He reserved a special hug for Roddy MacDonald, who emerged as the giant of the side that day. But it was a restrained Stein by comparison with old. The triumph of emerging alive from the wreckage on the A74 seemed to have given him a new perspective on his own life, and particularly on the

professional side of it. Perhaps football's triumphs now seemed more fleeting. His pleasure seemed to be derived not so much from beating Rangers (although that could never induce pain), but from having shown the sceptics who had thought the crash would finish him that he still had it in his power to engineer victories.

He appeared at the track-side briefly for a television interview, and then I watched him limp heavily back up the tunnel into a darker and more uncertain future. For that Cup victory that day was the last major prize he was ever to win in club football. The next year, without Kenny Dalglish who had moved to Liverpool, proved to be a disaster for him; he won nothing. He was replaced at the end of that season by Billy McNeill. As Stein himself once said to me: 'We all end up yesterday's men in this business. You're very quickly forgotten.' It was one of the few things he ever uttered that could be greeted with a resounding chorus of dissent.

A Stein grin broader than Hampden Park. The smile was never quite the same again

CHAPTER ELEVEN

THE
TEN
COMMANDERS

It is doubtful if the outbreak of World War Three would have produced a diversionary interest among Scots in the summer of 1978 when the international team went to Argentina for the World Cup. Ally MacLeod had fanned bushfires of nationalistic fervour which, in retrospect, can be seen to have raged out of control, but which at the time caused no concern even to those of us who were close to the phenomenon. Our euphoria seemed to excite some senses but dull others. We certainly could not detect the aroma of our own credibility being singed; not for a while, anyway.

Out there in the pampas, if we were not heady with expectation we were retiring to our rooms feeling like Abe Lincoln's negro boy who had stubbed his toe in the dark: we were too old to cry but it was too painful to laugh. That is why, as the national psyche had developed an acute obsession with success in the World Cup, the news of John Greig and Billy McNeill becoming respectively managers of Rangers and Celtic within days of one another tended to be swamped by other events. Normally the going of a man of Stein's stature and record, to be replaced by his alter ego on the field, and the sudden departure from a club he had loved since a boy by Jock Wallace, would have dominated press and television coverage for weeks. But when we heard the news in Cordoba it was pushed aside almost as an irrelevance, as if the captain of an expeditionary force had been informed that they had changed the cooks back at base.

The selection of Billy McNeill as successor to Stein could hardly have come about as a result of much soul-searching on the part of the Celtic board. He was the natural heir. Certainly he had proclaimed his great satisfaction with his job as manager at Aberdeen, if for no other reason than that he liked the chairman, Dick Donald, and the north-eastern environment. His family had discovered to their delight that there was life after the west of Scotland, to which they had thought themselves naturally disposed. But out of earshot of the acrimonious ambience of the Old Firm, from which as a family they were not immune either in the streets or supermarkets, they found a new lease of life. But however much he expressed his enjoyment at being at Pittodrie it was difficult to see him resisting the call from Parkhead when it came. And, of course, he didn't.

Jock Wallace, who had just taken Rangers to a second treble at the beginning of May, left the club suddenly. He has remained silent about the reason for his departure from an institution that meant so much to him. It certainly was not an act of wanton desertion. I believe he left because his independence as team manager did not fully exist, and also because his relationship with a man against whom even yet he would not dare say a word, Willie Waddell, had become stormy and ultimately untenable. You do not leave a triumphant Rangers for Leicester City unless for extremely compelling reasons. Wallace, despite his reputation for being a hard man, is in fact someone who makes friends much more easily than he does enemies, and who prefers it that way. He had not exhausted his professional expertise at Ibrox; only his patience.

John Greig was appointed manager of the club on 24 May 1978, six years to the very day he had captained Rangers to win the European Cup Winners' Cup in Barcelona. Unlike Billy McNeill, Greig had no managerial experience and that was immediately identified as a possible Achilles heel. But he brought to the job intelligence, humour and a remarkable capacity to put up with the 'slings and arrows of outrageous fortune'. He hid his wounds better than most.

It was suggested at the time that, because Rangers had made the Greig appointment, Celtic had in some way aped them by calling in McNeill. In fact, the timing was much less important than the fact that the line of succession was the right one for Celtic. McNeill had been helped, of course, by his time spent working on a shoestring at Shawfield with Clyde and then with an immensely professional organisation at Aberdeen. He was quite clearly better prepared for the job than ever John Greig had been.

When he brought Aberdeen to play Rangers in the Scottish Cup Final of 1978, McNeill stood beside me at the mouth of the tunnel, surveying the scene dominated by the legions of Rangers supporters who, as usual, were sending choruses heavenwards. 'I wish we had that sort of backing,' he said ruefully. Later he admitted that even some of the most experienced Aberdeen players had been beaten before a ball had been kicked, in part intimidated by the preponderance of sound emanating from the Rangers supporters. McNeill even then was missing the notably different dimension of the Old Firm.

Greig wanted to change Rangers. They had been successful under Jock Wallace, but only within the boundaries of Scotland. Their tactics had been parochial. Greig wished to put the emphasis on more skilful possession football, which would be more European than ever before. When he had claimed the scalps of both Juventus and PSV Eindhoven in the first part of the season, those sceptical of the right of this young manager to be in charge of one of Europe's great clubs began to take him and his side more seriously. Colin Jackson, Rangers' international centre-half, recognised Greig's efforts to change the club.

> I remember John Greig's team talks before the Juventus match in Italy. They were superb. He had done his homework in a way that none of us had been accustomed to. He got it absolutely right. He was spot on in the way he analysed each of our opponents and the general way they would play. He told us exactly how to cope with them playing in their own stadium, and it worked perfectly. We had never really had that amount of painstaking preparation before, and we relished it.'

Billy McNeill had been bequeathed a team which had sunk to the kind of mediocrity to which, as a Celt under Stein, he had hardly been accustomed. Some of his early post-match comments drew deeply on indignation as he spoke of men not really fit to be wearing the colours. He then bought Murdo

MacLeod from Dumbarton and Davy Provan from Kilmarnock, and hardly for a moment in the rest of his career would he come to regret that. But at first they could only remain in Rangers' jet stream as their old rivals eliminated them in a highly controversial League Cup semi-final that went into extra time and saw two men, Miller of Rangers and Burns of Celtic, sent off as they went down 2–3. And by Christmas the League flag also looked to be heading towards Ibrox.

Then Scottish football seized up. Temperatures plummeted and pitches froze, causing havoc with the fixture list. Celtic could not play their first game of 1979 until 3 March. Rangers, heading for the quarter-finals of the European Cup, were even bigger casualties of the congestion. As the thaw came the games began to flow, and moving into an extended season Rangers beat Aberdeen in a postponed League Cup Final, were knocked out of Europe by Cologne, beat Celtic 1–0 at Hampden on 5 May in a League game played there because of the reconstruction at Ibrox, and moved into a three-game Scottish Cup Final with Hibernian, which added to the enormous strain on them. Celtic, having apparently benefited from the long enforced winter break, had stormed back into contention for the Championship by winning three consecutive League games as Rangers continued their Cup saga with Hibs, thus preventing them from playing their League fixtures. The last Old Firm meeting was then scheduled for the evening of Monday 21 May. What it boiled down to was that if Celtic, now three points clear but having played two more games, won the match they would lift the Championship. Rangers, on the other hand, needed only a draw to bring them a giant step closer to gaining their second successive treble of League, League Cup and Scottish Cup. They, perhaps more than their rivals, were feeling the strain, as Colin Jackson recalls.

'The congestion towards the end of the season was incredible, and I think players were beginning to shade off because of the number of games we had played. But there was another factor. I think some of the older players in the side were taking too much criticism from the press. They couldn't get rid of us quickly enough, in fact. And I believe John was paying them too much attention. I think it was becoming clearer that he wanted rid of some of us, and when you think of how long and how well Sandy Jardine was to play after he left Rangers you can see that perhaps John was placing the emphasis of change in the wrong direction. So there was definitely some aggro between him and some of the more experienced players at a time when they in fact were holding the side together. It wasn't an ideal situation for us.'

That Monday evening held fair. The sap was rising in more than just the trees of Glasgow Green as buses rolled in from all over the country until a crowd of over 50 000 was inside Celtic Park. Alec Miller was among the Rangers players called for a light training session at the Albion ground that mid-afternoon before the game.

'We tried out one or two things and then John announced the team. I suppose it's easy enough now to talk about it, but I think it was the wrong team. It was to be 4–3–3. I think maybe we should have played 4–2–4 and dropped Davy Cooper to give us a bit more strength, because remember we only

Acute embarrassment never nullifies an own goal, which Colin Jackson discovered in finding his own net for Celtic's third goal

Booked

Every Celtic player was outstanding. But I would single out Aitken, McCluskey, MacLeod, McAdam and Provan as the miracle men on this history-making night for a Celtic team who three months ago would never have forecast themselves as champions.

Despite the pressures of the game, it was well controlled by referee Pringle.

As well as sending off Doyle he took the names of Aitken and McCluskey (Celtic) and Parlane, Jardine and Jackson (Rangers).

Poor Jackson. His booking came just a few seconds before his own goal, which helped to put Celtic striding to the front of Scottish soccer and into the European Cup next season.

TEAMS

THE TOP

	P	W	D	L	F	A	Pt
Celtic	36	21	6	9	61	37	48
Dundee United	36	18	8	10	56	37	44
Rangers	34	17	9	8	50	33	43
Aberdeen	36	13	14	9	59	36	40

It's the big turnaround. Above: Colin Jackson suffers after turning the ball into his own net for Celtic's third goal. Below: It's torment for Celtic as MacDonald opens the scoring

---

21 May 1979	Celtic 4 Rangers 2	Celtic Park
	(League match)	

Celtic: Latchford, McGrain, Lynch, Aitken, McAdam, Edvaldsson, Provan, Conroy (Lennox), McCluskey, MacLeod, Doyle

Rangers: McCloy, Jardine, Dawson, Johnstone, Jackson, MacDonald, McLean (Miller), Russell, Parlane, Smith, Cooper

Scorers: Aitken (66), McCluskey (74), Jackson (83, o.g.), MacLeod (90); MacDonald (9), Russell (76)

Referee: E. Pringle (Edinburgh)   *att*: 52 000

---

needed a point. I also recall Gordon Smith had a thigh injury but said he was fit to play. I don't think he was, because he struggled throughout the game. Anyway, when we got to Celtic Park it was packed as usual, but there was a frightening kind of atmosphere, very tense. It was a lovely night as well, I remember that. We scored first through Alec MacDonald. Davy Cooper actually set it up by beating two men and sweeping the ball over for Alec to knock it past Latchford. That was only after about ten minutes or so. We went in at half-time leading by that goal, but to be honest we weren't playing well. Our passing was terrible and despite the scoreline Celtic had really dominated the game. I remember John at half-time going round us all trying to impress on us that it wasn't good enough. We might have been one up, but he wasn't too happy at that stage.'

Curiously, as Davy Provan recalls, in the Celtic dressing-room Billy McNeill was being optimistic despite the scoreline and, although they were eager to get out again, when they did it was to head straight for apparent disaster.

❝ I almost felt sick when Johnny Doyle was sent off ten minutes into the second half. I have to say in retrospect that he was stupid to have kicked Alec

This tackle by Jackson annoyed Doyle. Doyle later annoyed the referee

Roy Aitken finds Peter McCloy's hands are quick on the draw

MacDonald, who was lying on the ground. But I also remember that when Doyle reached out with his hand to help him up, Alec snatched his hand away aggressively and I think it was that which sparked off the kick, although, as I say, it was rash. I don't know quite what it was – anger, or just that there was nothing to lose – but we just threw away all the tactical planning we had in our minds and pushed players forward with almost gay abandon, leaving ourselves very exposed at the back. We were honestly playing like a schoolboy team chasing after every ball, running everywhere. I remember finding myself at left back on one occasion tackling Bobby Russell, for example. It didn't seem to make sense, but we just got carried away with the fact that even though we had only ten men we seemed to be controlling the game.'

They were. In a flowing sortie up field in the sixty-sixth minute, Roy Aitken turned in a flick across goal by Davy Provan to make the score 1–1. Provan now began to think anything was possible.

⚽   I had played in three previous Old Firm games and had never been on the winning side, and there is nothing more depressing than that, believe you me. Now here we were feeling as if things were happening. About ten minutes after that I nearly came out of my skin. We were really running Rangers ragged and big Roy hit a shot at goal which was blocked and came out to George McCluskey, who just hammered it into the net. We chased him and almost suffocated him. We were in the lead 2–1. But you can imagine how we felt two minutes later when Davy Cooper sent in a corner and Bobby Russell swept it past Peter Latchford to make it 2–2. As the manager said afterwards, we had a second mountain to climb. Just after that Roy had a great header which was brilliantly saved by Peter McCloy, and I remember thinking to myself that we were going to go so far but no further and it was just going to be another of these games which would slip away from us.'

Colin Jackson, though, had an inadvertent part to play in Celtic pulling themselves back up again. He remembers the moment with a degree of pain.

⚽   Peter McCloy came out for a McCluskey cross and just got to it. But I was moving towards goal and I couldn't get out of the way of the ball. It hit me on the shoulder and went straight into the net. They said afterwards I headed it in. But it was more inelegant than that, and I think that won the game for them.'

Even now, leading by 3–2, Davy Provan was not so sure.

⚽   All right, we were in the lead, but with only ten men. I couldn't believe that Rangers wouldn't come back at us again. Then just before the final whistle Murdo MacLeod picked up the ball and moved towards the penalty area. I was way out to his left screaming for a pass, because I wanted to take the ball to the corner flag and do a bit of time wasting. But Murdo didn't even look at me. He just lashed out and the ball flashed into the net. It was a glorious finish, 4–2. People keep saying to me it was a pity the game wasn't covered by television, but I think it simply meant that people have their special memories of it that they'll enjoy even more. Murdo's last goal, for example, is now part of the folklore. He's now being credited with scoring it from almost his own half instead of 18 yards as it was. So television would have spoiled the enjoyment of the stories told about that game. Needless to say, the champagne was flowing in the dressing-room and Desmond White, the chairman, came down and said quite emotionally to us that it was the club's greatest occasion since Lisbon.'

As the Celtic supporters became engulfed in their own celebrations, the Rangers players felt as if they had been steam-rollered. Alec Miller grieved.

6 I am not a drinker so I couldn't even have the consolation of getting drunk, but it was without doubt the worst night I ever spent in my life.'

Colin Jackson sought solitude.

6 I went off on my own after the game and stopped at a pub I'd never been in before. I just sat glumly and met another couple of Rangers supporters who looked as stunned as me. We went back to their house and had a good drink. We've been friends ever since. It's surprising what adversity brings you.'

Celtic had won the Championship, the first of three that Billy McNeill was to pick up in his first spell as manager. Rangers had to be content with the League Cup and Scottish Cup double. It had been a good season, in fact, for John Greig, but after that night he was never quite the same again. The new equilibrium that he tirelessly sought to achieve at Ibrox had been upset and was never regained. Rangers were not to win the title for another eight years and Greig lasted only another four at the club, his own civilities and belief in attractive, attacking football swamped by the outcry of the supporters for the success that it seemed would forever elude him.

Celtic had grabbed a glory enhanced by the timing of the game and the circumstances in which a handicap had in fact become a prime asset, moving players to heights they themselves could barely appreciate afterwards. Far from miraculous, it was immensely human. Like a mother who might single-handedly lift a car to free her trapped child and wonder in retrospect how it had been achieved, so the performances of the Celtic players defied natural explanation but hinted at the power of the spirit over the flesh. It was a lesson for us all.

The end of a game, the starting-blocks for the celebrations as Billy McNeill and co seek their heroes

CHAPTER TWELVE

GOALS AND AIMS

In the early part of the 1980s Rangers and Celtic playing together were beginning to look like some vaudeville duo who could not yet believe that the day of the soft-shoe shuffle was over and that their kind of theatre was being eclipsed by counter-attractions. The younger upstarts in the business were beginning to divert attention away from Glasgow to other parts of the land where the term 'provincial' was coming to be interpreted merely as a point on the compass and not as a mark of the second-rate. Alec Ferguson at Aberdeen and Jim McLean at Dundee United had begun to nudge the Old Firm off the stage.

A European trophy had come to Aberdeen along with domestic Cup and League honours. Dundee United had won a Championship and a couple of League Cups and had confounded Europe by proving that humble origins need not be a handicap when they reached the semi-final of the European Champions Cup. All this lent a curious look to Scottish football, conditioned as it was to Glasgow setting the fashion, and one writer had the temerity to suggest a title for the north-east clubs: the 'New Firm'. If not an offence against copyright, it was at least an affront to the establishment and more than a hint that the new phenomenon was anything but transient.

As season 1985–6 unwound, therefore, David Hay and Jock Wallace, the current managers of Celtic and Rangers, could hardly have been unaware of the growing discontent in their neck of the woods, for on top of the north-east challenge a new power had emerged: Hearts. Despite at the start having been considered 200–1 outsiders to win the Championship, they were now beginning to look eminently capable of doing exactly that. As the Old Firm approached their meeting of 22 March 1986 it looked distinctly possible that for the first time since 1955 neither club would end the season with a major trophy.

The industrial depression hitting the west of Scotland was hardly calculated to encourage people to throw their money away on indifferent entertainment at Parkhead or Ibrox. Gartcosh steel plant had just closed. Unemployment was setting in like an incurable virus all around the traditional heavy industrial areas from which the great bulk of the Old Firm support came. Normally a Saturday football break would have acted like a tonic, if not an absolute antidote, against the rigours of job loss and the uncertainty it brought in its wake, but the Old Firm supporters were not enjoying that kind of therapy. Looking back to November of 1985 it was noted that during that month the two clubs had hardly registered a victory between them. And as their meeting in March loomed, greater publicity was given to the Hearts–Hibs clash. Rangers had lost touch in the League race, but Celtic, with a number of games in hand, statistically stood a chance of catching Hearts. Nobody at that stage outside Celtic Park itself paid too much attention to the relative positions of both clubs. Most were simply focusing on the Hearts renaissance.

As a result, life was easy for neither Jock Wallace nor David Hay. Wallace had been third choice for the Rangers job after Alec Ferguson, whose rejection of the post was based greatly on his family's distaste for the religious overtones of football in Glasgow, and Jim McLean, who rejected it even though he had been encouraged by Jock Stein to accept. Wallace, for his part, was so desperate to return to Ibrox it would not have mattered if he had been thirtieth choice. As manager of Motherwell he had walked on to Fir Park one Saturday afternoon to be greeted like the prodigal by the Rangers supporters who then gave him a long ovation, much to the embarrassment of the then Rangers manager, John Greig, sitting in the visitors' dug-out.

There is little doubt that Wallace had more than the welfare of Motherwell Football Club at heart when he suddenly returned from Leicester City. At one stage after Greig's departure, when Rangers had apparently reached a dead-end in finding a successor, Jock said to me in a sudden fit of candour, 'Why don't they just lift the phone and talk to me? What's wrong with them?' Rangers were picking their way carefully, because they felt they could not afford to make a mistake after the failure of John Greig. The only reservation they had about Wallace was that they might be turning back the hands of the clock. They had even distantly sounded out John Lyall of West Ham, who at least could claim a Scottish connection through his grandparents. He told Rangers quite frankly that he could not accept being tied by their unwritten but nevertheless *de facto* policy of signing only Protestants. So they would, in any case, soon have been running out of options. They knew, too, that there was a popular groundswell for Wallace. Late one evening, after weeks of conjecture, I received a phone call from Jock. He simply sang, 'Follow, Follow', the Rangers song, over the phone. I made the not too profound assumption that he had again become Rangers manager.

By comparison with the ebullient Wallace, David Hay was a model of self-restraint. Celtic midfield player Murdo MacLeod, signed from Dumbarton by Billy McNeill, knew he was much tougher than this, however.

> **6** I know Davy's public image was of a very soft-spoken and very mannerly man. But he could ram home his points effectively when necessary. Woe betide anybody who roused him. He could slam into us as effectively as anybody, although he was admittedly a bit laid back most of the time by comparison with Billy McNeill.'

Publicly, though, he seemed at times incredibly passive. On occasions when you would have thought he would have been in the mood to chew up media people after a difficult game with an adverse result, he would simply puff earnestly on a cheroot and talk softly as if there was little he could do to control the fates which govern us all. It is a comment on the nature of management in the modern age that this civilised side of him seemed inadequate to those who felt that Celtic were in decline. As a consequence, he was in trouble.

Rangers' comeback
starts from Cammy
Fraser's head

Nevertheless, Hay's predicament was a bed of roses compared to that of Jock Wallace. The man who had vowed he would make Rangers great again and who had said with sincerity to me, 'If I ever leave this place again I'll have to be carried out feet first,' was simply not delivering. His good intentions, his unstinting devotion to the club and his enormous capacity for work were getting Rangers no nearer winning the prize they coveted above all else, the League Championship. During this second spell as Rangers manager he had won two League Cups but never at any significant stage of that period did the club look like being contenders for the League title. Even the marvellous rapport he had developed with supporters, and which he still treasures, was beginning to come under strain as people both outside and within the club began to feel that Rangers were marking time while the rest of the world was moving on. Wallace knew he had supporters on the board who saw in him something of the right pedigree that would in due course pay dividends. But it was the wrong sort of belief. It was not that Rangers would never win anything but nothing in the preoccupation with terracing traditions and the concentration on muscle and lung power to the detriment of the skills of the game could suggest a proper format for the future that would generate even more success. It is one thing to be strong and fit but it is another when you are expending that energy by simply marking time. But Wallace was also aware of a new thinking personified by the most recent appointment to the Ibrox board, a direct contact of the club's owner, Lawrence Marlborough. His name was David Holmes. The empty seats on most match days at Ibrox in their magnificent stadium were beginning to offend the eyes of Holmes most grievously. For many weeks before that last Old Firm match on 22 March he had determined that this state of affairs could not go on for ever. It was just a matter of choosing exactly the right time to act.

---

22 March 1986   **Rangers 4   Celtic 4**   Ibrox Stadium
(League Match)

Rangers: Walker, Burns (D. Ferguson). Munro, McPherson, McKinnon, Durrant, McMinn (Cooper), Russell, Fleck, Fraser, McCoist

Celtic: Bonner, W. McStay, Whyte, Aitken, O'Leary, MacLeod, McClair, P. McStay (McInally), Johnston, Burns, Archdeacon (Grant)

Scorers: Fraser (36,64), McCoist (53), Fleck (58); Johnston (21), McClair (29), Burns (48), MacLeod (70)

Referee: D. Syme (Rutherglen)   *att*: 41 000

The two managers sitting in the dug-outs might well have felt as if they were in air-raid shelters instead, for they were under attack from all quarters and they would have been very short-sighted indeed if they had not realised there was more than a distinct possibility that they were facing the sack in the not too distant future. But if Jock Wallace was aware of any pressure directly from above, he did not show it, as Ally McCoist particularly recalls.

Celtic caught, not only on
the hop, but also in the act
of dissent as Fraser puts
Rangers in the lead

He was the same as ever. Cheerful, optimistic, still full of life. I actually loved the man because he did a great deal for me personally. Before he came I felt

I was just drifting along getting nowhere fast, but he spent a great deal of time with me talking about my game and it brought me on, there's no doubt about that. However, I have to admit the team was in a rut. I can't tell you how awful it is to play in that great stadium with only eight or nine thousand there. But that's what was happening as the attendances just plummeted. We were really struggling at times and I couldn't see how we could turn the corner, and yet before this Old Firm game Big Jock had never passed on any anxieties to us. To him it was just another chance to beat *them*.'

Murdo MacLeod of Celtic felt more confident.

❛ Everybody had their eyes on Hearts but we knew we could still possibly catch them, so that was a great incentive to us, while Rangers had only their pride to play for, and of course I know about that since I know Rangers supporters well. My family came from that tradition and people always ask me how I felt playing against a team I had supported as a boy. That's an easy one. It was great. Celtic asked me to sign, whereas Rangers didn't; it's as simple as that. Now the Celtic supporters knew I gave them one hundred per cent and so I got on well with them. But I never really experienced trouble from Rangers supporters. They knew what my background was, I suppose. In fact, some Celtic supporters wondered why I seemed so friendly with the Rangers players. They had watched the game on television and as I ran from the tunnel I patted Davy McKinnon, the Rangers full-back, on the backside – just a kind of goodwill gesture to my own cousin. It was noted. I think if I had had a bad game that would have been brought up in evidence.'

The new Ibrox stadium stood steadfast against a torrential downpour which saturated the pitch but did nothing to dampen the ardour of supporters, whose throats were largely immune to the elements. The initial shouting came principally from the Celtic end. Murdo MacLeod remembers the match.

❛ What a start! Two goals up in half an hour. They were the first two real shots we had on goal in that time but they counted, and frankly I felt we were going to run away from them. I remember I half-hit a shot (unlike me of course) after Owen Archdeacon had sent it over, and just as I thought we had made a hash of it Mo Johnston slipped it into the net. They pressed a bit after that but I never felt we were going to give much away. Then just about on the half-hour Owen crossed again towards me, but as the ball went loose Brian McClair stepped in and hit it in. Now it looked plain sailing then, but what changed the whole game and I suppose made it the great match it will always be remembered as was the sending off of Willie McStay.'

McStay had been booked early in the game for paying undue attention to the legs of the gangling winger Ted McMinn, whose eccentricities could admittedly dement almost any full-back. Just after Celtic went two up he repeated a scything tackle on the winger and was promptly asked to leave by the referee. Two minutes later, against the ten men, Rangers pulled one back, laid on for Cammy Fraser by Ally McCoist, to make it 2–1.

> I was out on the left, looked up and swept it over for Cammy Fraser to head it in. Now we knew we were playing against ten men and sometimes that can inspire the handicapped side but I just felt we might get back into it. I get on well with Roy Aitken, the Celtic captain, and the banter between us can be great, but out on the field the rivalry between us is fierce, I can tell you. So here we were trying to fight back and beginning to look good when Tommy Burns scored for Celtic right after the interval. I think he put it in from about fifteen yards. Big Roy shouted at me, 'Hey, McCoist. How about that then? Right through the middle of your defence. Three–one.' I knew the score all right. I kind of hid. But not long after that I scored one of the best goals I've ever scored. All I can recall is picking up the ball from Davy McKinnon and turning towards goal. I sensed the tackles coming at me but I kept jinking, and just when I felt I had it really under control I let fly with my right foot. It hardly rose from the ground. It was about 25 yards out and I think it got a bit of help from the greasy surface. When I saw it go in and started to run round the penalty area with Rangers players chasing me to hug me, they could hardly catch me because I was trying to find Roy Aitken. 'How about *that?*' I said to him. 'Three–two.' But that's nothing to what I said when we scored again!'

Robert Fleck pulled Rangers level when he picked up a rebound from Derek Whyte and scored from close range. The rain had long since been forgotten as one of the most entertaining Old Firm games ever see-sawed almost recklessly towards a fitting climax. After 64 minutes, when Cammy Fraser scored his second, it looked as if the ten-man Celtic team, who appeared to have put themselves beyond reach in the first half-hour, were sunk. But Murdo MacLeod was never the type to surrender that easily.

> When Rangers went into the lead we were all back defending. There's no doubt about it, they were giving us some stick thereabouts. They were pounding down at us. We just couldn't stop that fourth goal. A header came in from about the 18-yard line and there was Cammy Fraser to turn it over the line. For the first time in the game we were behind. But I'll never forget what happened then. I think it was about twenty minutes to go and the rain was driving against us. Mo Johnston slipped the ball into my path and I hit with everything I knew from 25 yards and saw it soaring towards the net. It's a great sight when you see a shot like that going in.'

Ally McCoist remembers:

> When I saw the equaliser I knew big Roy would make for me to rub it in. He did, but I didn't see him for I just pulled up my jersey out of my shorts and

The rain did not diminish the enthusiasm of Burns and Munro

covered my face and ran back to the centre circle. Still, it was a great game. Eight goals shared. Two fight-backs. You don't mind a draw in those circumstances.'

There had been some ridiculously bad defensive play by both sides in the squally conditions, but at the end of the ninety minutes the game's technical deficiencies were overlooked by two sets of supporters who stood around the stands of Ibrox and roared their approval as the muddied teams dragged themselves off the pitch back into the dressing-rooms. Both sides derived great satisfaction from the result. Celtic, having played so long with ten men, had survived. Rangers, twice two goals behind, had saved themselves a threatening indignity. It was an unusual event to have both sets of supporters leaving the stadium in high spirits, as if each were claiming the honours. It left one with the feeling that this world would be a much safer and more enlightened place if all Old Firm games ended up as high-scoring draws.

Yet that feeling was not universally held. In the Ibrox boardroom after the match, when the Celtic directors had departed the scene, there was much jubilation. One man could not understand this feeling because, as he saw it, Rangers had merely gained a draw at home playing against ten men. The elation did not seem appropriate. So, when Jock Wallace made the statement that this was the sort of stuff the punters loved, David Holmes challenged him.

Scottish ballet à la Old Firm. The ball meanwhile is redundant

Here's mud in your eye.
Tommy Burns in the Mack
Sennet push away. Ally
McCoist not seeing the
funny s

'Sorry,' he said. 'It's not what the punters love at all. They would really have loved us to win. That's what it's all about.' Wallace took issue with this, but he was on to a loser in taking on Holmes. The man had made up his mind that enough was enough. He told the owner, Lawrence Marlborough, that he could not go on under these circumstances. Marlborough immediately offered him the running of the club, which he accepted. Within three weeks of that date he had effectively taken over power at Ibrox, sacked Jock Wallace and three directors and presented the club with a new manager who sported a deep Italian tan.

CHAPTER THIRTEEN

THE OCTOBER REVOLUTION

Graeme Souness hailed originally from Edinburgh, but having seen out his adolescence amidst the lustrous attractions of London, served an apprenticeship in the north-east of England, matured in Merseyside and languished comfortably with Sampdoria in Italy, he was probably cosmopolitan enough to be ready for Glasgow by April 1986. It is possible that he had forgotten a remark made by Bill Shankly, who laid the foundation for the success at Anfield that Souness was later to enjoy. The Shanks, never wanting for a picturesque analogy, had once declared, 'A worse job than even managing Liverpool Football Club would be that of a debt collector in Glasgow.' Souness's status was to be somewhat better than that, however, and was to bring sufficient financial reward to soften the blow which he no doubt initially felt in having to give up a Mediterranean climate for one that can be a trifle harsher.

David Holmes, in his new powerful position, had acted swiftly after that last Old Firm game of season 1985–6. He called that day the 'catalyst'. The aggravations he had been feeling for some time had come to a head.

> There was a spell in December of 1985 when we had gone six games with only one victory and there were murmurs in the boardroom about having to get rid of Jock Wallace. If I heard it once I heard it a dozen times that things weren't working out. Then we came in for a game early in the New Year, I think it was. We beat Dundee 5–0. I couldn't believe the complacency that provoked. Everything that had been said in the previous few weeks was forgotten. We were back on the rails. Everything was hunky-dory. It was staring anybody in the face that this wasn't so. We were going nowhere fast.'

There was a clear contrast between this 'outsider' and the rest of the Ibrox directors, who were men brought up in the tradition of supporters of the club and who had worked patiently to attain their positions on the board. All were devoted. None slacked at their various tasks. But they could not fill Ibrox with supporters. Holmes was probably the only man among them who did not know by heart the words of the traditional Ibrox songs, and he had no intention of learning them. His contribution was to be that of master-builder, not choir-master. The old ways had to go.

In his new capacity as chief executive of the club, and fully backed by Marlborough from his self-imposed exile in Lake Tahoe in the States, Holmes swung into action. He phoned Souness and offered him the managership.

> I got this call asking me if I would be interested in becoming player-manager with Rangers. Player-manager wasn't such an unusual request because of what Kenny had done at Liverpool, and I knew without too much thinking

how big Rangers could be. Now, a lot of people have pointed to an interview I did on television on the day Jock Stein died, when somebody asked me if I would ever come back to Scotland in any capacity and I said there was only one club I would come back to and that Jock Wallace had better look out. I was being truly light-hearted and meant nothing by it. But, of course, some people assumed this had been a great strategy in my mind for all that time. It wasn't. I just weighed up what was said to me on the phone and agreed to meet David Holmes in London.'

By the time they had left their meeting in a hotel in London they had agreed terms, even though Souness still had eighteen months of his Italian contract to run. But more was to be done, as Holmes readily admits.

There had to be a clean-out. I had to have men on the board with me who would be on the same business wavelength and who would be much more realistic about the objectives of the club. So I went on a short break to Jersey and met Lawrence Marlborough again. He agreed there had to be boardroom sackings. When eventually I got round to asking the three directors to resign I knew I was dealing with people whose whole lives had practically revolved round the club and who were nice men. But I had to do it, to make our board more dynamic. When we did that the next thing was to try to rush through the details of Graeme's transfer to the club so that he could go to the World Cup in Mexico for Scotland with the name Glasgow Rangers behind him. Then we presented him to the media.'

In the space of three weeks Holmes had turned Ibrox upside down. Even those inured to the previous upheavals within the club were taken aback by the speed and the dimension of the changes that had been made. Souness himself came to look at the team and had to conclude that he had inherited one of the worst senior sides he had ever watched. He learned very quickly, too, how badly Rangers supporters felt watching Celtic succeed, which they had done dramatically at the end of that season by winning 5–0 against St Mirren at Love Street (while Hearts were losing 2–0 at Dundee) to snatch the title.

When I first came here I wanted to put the Rangers–Celtic thing into perspective. To me, winning two points against Celtic is the same as winning two points against Motherwell. I stand by that. I even said that I wouldn't mind losing four times to Celtic in a season so long as we won the Championship. Maybe in my first few steps as manager that was too naive, or perhaps too practical for our supporters. I think I know better now what the Old Firm game means. No disrespect to my old friends on Merseyside, but quite honestly the derby down there is nothing in comparison. Down there families will be split down the middle, one side supporting Everton, the other Liverpool, and you even see the colours mixing on the terraces. But not here. This is deadly serious by comparison and it influences everything in Scottish football.'

In the first Old Firm game of season 1986–7 at Ibrox, Rangers won by the only goal of the game, scored by Ian Durrant. David Holmes began to cast a more satisfied eye over his huge investment.

Rangers had been too parochial. We wanted to extend our vision, so I was whole-heartedly behind Graeme going out and signing Terry Butcher and Chris Woods to start off with. They were big names and they cost a lot of money. But that's the way we had to travel.'

On 26 October Souness and his English imports were to face up to their first Old Firm final, the Skol Cup at Hampden Park. It was a Sunday and the game was to be televised live throughout Scotland.

26 October 1986 **Rangers 2   Celtic 1** Hampden Park
(Skol Cup Final)

Rangers: Woods, Nicholl, Munro, Fraser (MacFarlane), Dawson, Butcher, Ferguson, McMinn, McCoist (Fleck), Durrant, Cooper

Celtic: Bonner, Grant, MacLeod, Aitken, Whyte, McGhee (Archdeacon), McClair, McStay, Johnston, Shepherd, McInally

Scorers: Durrant (62), Cooper (84, pen.); McClair (70)

Referee: D. Syme (Rutherglen)   *att*: 74 219

Souness, unfit, sat initially in the stand.

❏ It was very frustrating not being fit to play, and in fact I wondered how I was going to put up with just sitting there watching. I never like to see the start of a game, so I deliberately hold back. I heard the roar of the crowd at the first whistle and knew it had started. That seemed to give me the nerve to go through the door and up to my seat. Thereafter I was too involved with what was happening out there to know whether or not I was nervous.'

There is no overture to an Old Firm game. No one is allowed the luxury of an opening few minutes of grace in which you can perhaps find your feet or sense the mood of the opposition or the idiosyncrasies of the pitch. The atmosphere invites instant involvement, and the opening of most of these games is like a floodgate being released on a huge draught of nervous energy. On that grey afternoon there was a particular intensity to this feeling because in the background lurked the notion that Celtic were the only club in the country who could stop the Ibrox momentum from developing into a runaway juggernaut, and that perhaps they could do it all inside ninety minutes. I am sure Celtic not only wanted to win a cup, but felt also they could burst a bubble. More realistically, on this game depended not so much the viability of the Rangers revolution but the pace at which it was likely to develop in the future. Celtic, on the other hand, not noted for profligacy of spending, desperately wanted to show that success could be achieved by traditional and more modest means. The game was therefore laden with all kinds of possible consequences.

To the two English internationals this was a particular test of character, for while they had been blooded to a certain extent in the previous League encounter, this after all was a Cup Final and they were seeing the full extent and power of the huge Celtic support for the first time. In addition, there were more than a few wishing to brand them as nothing more than footballing mercenaries. Terry Butcher, in fact, claims to have been sanguine about the whole affair.

❏ We really settled in quickly in Scotland considering we knew nothing about the place and, indeed, had some unfounded prejudices against it. The people were great. Certainly some Celtic supporters would give you stick, but that's

just part of the business. So that day at Hampden I think I had had enough education about what it all meant to everybody. The hype was unbelievable and that meant we were rightly geared up for the day.'

The first half did not excite the imagination greatly, although a shot at either end, one by Maurice Johnston, the other by Cammy Fraser, hit posts. The second half had a distinctly different character. It started with a rush by Celtic, as if they felt they had been shadow-boxing up till then. Chris Woods had an outstanding save as he somersaulted backwards into the net, tipping a ball which looked as if it might slip in just over the bar. Butcher rose persistently to head away from Maurice Johnston, and beside him Ally Dawson, a man who must have realised he had no real future at Ibrox and who had been drafted in that day for the suspended Dave McPherson, was playing as if he was on permanent contract. In short, the Rangers defence was holding out in a way which must have been frustrating Celtic. The pressure was there, but the reality was that Celtic were simply bouncing off a defence that was beginning to look sounder by the minute. This is a well-known formula for the scoring of a goal at the other end, and Rangers obliged. Terry Butcher viewed it from nearby.

6 Ian Durrant is a marvellous player for getting into the box. His runs behind people are some of the best in the game. So when Peter Grant fouled Davy Cooper and we got a free kick, I went up for it. I rose in the air with Roy and I'm not exactly sure how the ball broke to Ian but he suddenly flashed through on the left side of me and smashed it past Pat Bonner. I remember he jumped over the advertising hoardings in delight, and I went after him.'

Durrant's pleasure at scoring was not based on the knowledge that he had just won for himself from the sponsor a free trip on Concorde for being the opening scorer, but that he had just notched his second goal against Celtic in successive games and that, coming as it did almost half-way through the second half, it was a more than useful contribution.

It took Celtic only eight minutes to equalise, however. More than a goal, it was a magnificently structured gesture of defiance. Aitken to McClair in midfield, the ball pushed through to Mo Johnston on the edge of the box for the one-two which, placed perfectly in front of McClair, went from his right foot to the roof of the net like a stone out of a sling. It seemed like an assertion of superiority; but it was not to last, and the game entered a phase which would practically blot out of memory all that had gone beforehand. Terry Butcher was central to it.

Celtic's only response. A Brian McClair blast goes in

> Let's face it, I've watched the replay of this a countless number of times and there can never be any other conclusion than that it was a penalty kick. Of course, you'll get a different story from Roy Aitken. But as I see it I followed the flight of the ball from Derek Ferguson's free kick towards the far post. Roy and I had had tussles all afternoon and we were certainly in close contact as we made our way across the penalty area, but I was definitely pushed in the back and went down. When I got up, the referee had awarded a penalty. There was a lot of arguing going on around him and the kick was delayed for what seemed like an eternity. When Davy Cooper walked back to take it I turned away and looked down towards the Celtic end and just listened. I

Possession is nine-tenths of the law. But penalties come from grabbing

Johnston sent off. Celtic's last hopes vanish

hadn't the nerve to watch. When I heard the roar I turned and saw the ball in the net, and with so little time left I knew we had won the Cup.'

There were six minutes left, during which the game degenerated into a mixture of farce and undignified squabble. Four minutes after Rangers had gone into the lead Mo Johnston and Stuart Munro clashed on the touchline. Both were booked, Munro for kicking an opponent and Johnston for apparently making at least an attempt to head-butt his opponent. As the Celtic player had already been carded it meant he had to be ordered off. It is here that we have to distort the historical perspective considerably. Emboldened by such as Voltaire who once declared, 'History is a pack of tricks we play on the dead,' we have to move on from that moment when Mo Johnston ran from the pitch in anger, betraying his feelings with a genuflection that had as much to do with religion as an entreaty to come and have a fight. For in truth he was displaying solidarity with the Celtic masses at one end of the ground and realised full well that blessing himself would make a two-fingered gesture to the Rangers supporters seem like an ecumenical initiative. We move on from that explosive moment to that bizarre morning of 10 July 1989 when he sat encapsulated in red white and blue in the heart of Ibrox as a newly signed Rangers player bought for £1.4 million, only a couple of months after it looked as if he would go back from Nantes in France to his great love Celtic.

Police attend a confrontation between referee David Syme and Celtic manager David Hay. No arrests ensued

Even yet to those ingrained in the ways of Glasgow and the two clubs it is difficult to superimpose one image on the other; the cradle Catholic exposing his bitter feelings against another club and the benign, red-haired freckled innocent sitting that morning almost three years later expressing his admiration for Graeme Souness. What we experienced that day was a quite

Souness nonchalant on bench. Hay in silent prayer in dug-out

unprecedented culture shock which almost numbed the senses. Up till then most of us had assumed that Rangers had staved off the fateful day of signing their first acknowledged Catholic by a mix of commercial and sporting success and the use of neatly timed statements of intent. There can be no doubting the sincerity of Holmes and Souness who had made it clear initially that they would not let the old prejudices get in their path as they strode into the future. But equally there is little doubt that both men hardened their views about Rangers as the reality of their tenure began to sink in. Eventually Holmes was to tell me, 'When we won the championship only three clubs sent us their congratulations. Basically they're jealous of us. Not in all my experience in all walks of life have I experienced the hatred of the kind that's directed towards this club. So nobody is going to tell us how to run our own affairs.'

At the same time Souness began to form the impression that a cabal sympathetic towards Celtic Park existed in the media who would belittle Rangers whenever they could. Real or imagined as that may have been these two innovative men began to strike a more closed-door attitude which aroused doubts as to whether they would ever break with tradition. The fact that Rangers decided to do so in a manner more akin to a great leap into the unknown, with a player who had once expressed to me his hatred of all

things blue, and which they must have known was bound to provoke bitter resentment on the other side of the city, is a testament to the remarkable lengths that Souness in particular was prepared to go to uproot the club from the arid soil of the past. By then Holmes had gone, replaced as the chairman by the new owner of the club David Murray who although new to the trade, as was Holmes when he started out, was nevertheless the derring-do sort of entrepreneur who would support the audacity of Souness in a matter like this.

None of us watching Rangers finally win 2–1 that October day almost three years previously could have anticipated the manner in which the club would dismantle the final barrier even though they had already made astounding changes within Scottish football. For instance, here was a country ravaged by industrial decline resulting in an appalling male unemployment rate of 42 per cent in the district of Govan (where Ibrox is sited), and an overall rate of 25 per cent in the west of Scotland. At the same time latent feelings for political independence were beginning to resurface. Yet within two years of bringing Souness to Ibrox, attendances at Scottish football matches had increased from 2 446 262 to a staggering 3 874 079 on the back of Rangers' importation of foreign talent. By creating this boom within an overall recession David Holmes had not only initiated a revolution but created an astonishing social paradox.

That Rangers, therefore, could take a major opponent from that Skol Cup Final day of bitterness and convert him to new colours was perhaps more the result of a combination of their ambition, their wealth and the natural avarice of the modern professional footballer rather than the emergence of a new moral code. But it would not have been possible if Holmes had not introduced Souness in the first place.

When Johnston walked into the famous Blue Room that morning in his red white and blue tie and navy blazer he not only shocked his old friends, and confounded those in the streets outside who did not want him as a friend; but also proved that Rangers, for whatever motives, were now free of the shackles of their own history and were embarked on a course from which there could be no returning.

CHAPTER FOURTEEN

HOMECOMING

To the vast majority of Celtic supporters the departure of Billy McNeill as manager of the club in June 1983 had all the civilised trappings of the St Valentine's Day massacre. Never before in the history of a club which had always prided itself on its discreet and private handling of its internal affairs had there been such a publicly muddied affair, and it gave the impression that Celtic and McNeill, far from being made for one another, were now sworn enemies for life. The clash between the manager and the chairman became too fundamental to be stored cosily within the confines of Celtic Park, largely because the issues, although more often than not spelled out in domestic terms (such as the dispute about the level of McNeill's salary and the information made public about his mortgage assistance), were more basically about the balance of power within the club and the efforts of the manager to be seen as being as powerful as his predecessor Jock Stein in the running of the club. McNeill, whether rightly or wrongly, at the time felt that his style was being cramped, largely by the authoritarian figure of the chairman, Desmond White, who ruled the club with considerable dignity but with an almost apostolic certitude in a Celtic chairman's right to overrule anything or anybody within the club. The clash became too much for both parties and McNeill left to take over at Manchester City, leaving behind a multitude of people who were not interested in the debating points raised between the warring factions but were simply baffled as to why a manager of outstanding ability and a pedigree so uniformly Celtic could have reached such a low that divorce was simply unavoidable.

Whoever might have been in the right in this dispute, there is little doubt that the only way Billy McNeill could have made himself unpopular with the Celtic following was to have asked for a job at Ibrox. Clearly sentiment was on his side as a letter to the *Glasgow Herald* at the time illustrated.

> Such have been our traditions and our deeply felt sense of family (a family to which Mr McNeill belonged for twenty-five years) that our anger cannot fully be expressed. The atmosphere of family has been destroyed, loyalty has been discarded, and our spirit of charity and tolerance has been dissipated into a meanness of spirit and servility to money that is deeply abhorrent.'

Even in retrospect, if those thoughts seem overstated one has to appreciate that overstatement has never been out of a place on a football terrace.

Billy McNeill was on reasonably familiar terms with adversity, however. A year earlier he had been employed by BBC Television as a commentator at the World Cup in Spain. One day we travelled together to Tony Dalli's restaurant near Puerto Banus to meet and interview Sean Connery. The two got on famously, and the interview went well but suddenly, out of the blue and out of context, Billy admitted that through no fault of his own he had been hit by a financial disaster in private business. The loss he mentioned took the breath away. Yet he continued to laugh and joke his way through the afternoon as if all that had happened was that someone had picked his pocket and relieved him of a tube of Smarties. Some of us, under similar circumstances, might simply have walked out to sea from the Marbella beach and not come back. But any suffering McNeill may have been experiencing was well hidden. This resilience was to be of immeasurable value to him throughout his period in English football.

David Hay, in similar fashion, treated the hard times like the good in such a uniquely imperturbable manner that, outside his outburst after the Skol Cup Final, Hay in defeat seemed almost indistinguishable from Hay in victory. For that reason alone he was immensely likeable, but even from the day he entered the portals of Celtic Park there were insiders who felt he simply was not up to the job. This, so far as the records show, was never articulated in a formal manner in the early days, but from time to time it was an undercurrent of private conversation as Celtic lurched from one disappointment to another. The dramatic winning of the League at Love Street on the very last day of season 1985–6 prolonged his professional life, but did not guarantee him long-term security in face of the coming of Souness and the age of big bucks which, combined, seemed to swamp Celtic and Hay simultaneously. The sacking of David Hay was left to the chairman of Celtic, Jack McGinn.

In the most practical sense we became interested in Billy McNeill when we learned of his sacking at Aston Villa in early May 1987. The board had then made up their minds that we would have to make a managerial change, not simply as a reaction to Rangers but because we just felt the club was slipping and getting out of control. Before we did anything about Davy we had to make sure about Billy's intentions. I knew he was in Glasgow this particular day staying with Mike Jackson the ex-Celtic player, so I phoned him there and asked if I could meet and talk to him. Now I know a great deal was made out of us meeting in a car park at Clydebank almost as if we were carrying out some sort of espionage. But really, at that stage how would it have looked if I had been seen walking through the front door of, say, the Albany Hotel with Billy? The speculation would have been rampant. And supposing things hadn't worked out. It would have been embarrassing. Where we actually met was a simple matter of geography, nothing more nor less. Half-way point, if you like. We sat in the car and I asked Billy if he would come back to Parkhead and he answered 'Yes' without any hesitation. Then he immediately asked, 'What about Davy?' I told him what we had to do. We didn't talk terms in any way and it was soon over. I contacted Davy Hay and asked to meet him at Celtic Park, which we did in the old boardroom. I told him it was the unanimous decision of the board that he had to go. His very first words were, 'I expected this.' Now nobody takes a sacking well, let's be honest. It was very difficult for me, but even more so for Davy, of course. I asked him if he would consider resigning. He said he would have to think about that. He also added that he felt it a pity that the entire board hadn't the courage to show up for his sacking. I could understand his feelings, but

how much better would it have been with a group of people there rather than just myself? It would have been much more messy. Anyway, when he returned he said that after talking it over with the family he had decided he wouldn't resign. But it was all over in any case, so he had to be sacked. We called a press conference for that afternoon and we revealed Billy as our new manager. It had all happened inside a day, but it was the best way of going about the matter. We acted in what we honestly believed to be the best possible interests of the club, and I think in retrospect that is how it turned out to be.'

McNeill was reminded almost immediately of his not too successful four-year exile in England.

A journalist wrote that I had come back to Celtic with the worst possible credentials for the job. No doubt he was thinking of England, but he had conveniently forgotten my record before I left Celtic when we won three titles under my management. That was a statement I wasn't likely to forget, and it was the sort of thing that reminded me of what I was facing. But apart from that I was just delighted to be back. I did have my low moments in England, although not everything was as black as some people painted it, but I never gave up hope of getting back even though it did seem very unlikely.'

If not exactly a return to Shangri-la, at least within a very few days we were seeing a totally rejuvenated McNeill. One had received an image of him from a television screen sitting in the dug-out at Villa as his team slumped towards relegation, looking tired and drawn as if he had come through an emotional mincing machine, and it seemed that his mistake of going to Villa had led him to premature ageing. Free of all this and back where he belonged, he quickly took on his former appearance and launched himself into the job by doing what was initially expected of him, entering the transfer market. He signed striker Andy Walker from Motherwell, Cornishman Chris Morris from Sheffield Wednesday and, perhaps most surprisingly of all at the time, thirty-year-old Billy Stark from Aberdeen. At that stage the Celtic supporters were too busy luxuriating in the thought of having McNeill back to bother making invidious comparisons with the lavish spending of Rangers. The right hand was on the till, and that was good enough. But clearly McNeill did not have the benefit of the Ibrox treasure trove. By comparison there was a look of creative improvisation about his first efforts to restructure the side.

> We had lost very experienced players like Mo Johnston, Brian McClair and Murdo MacLeod, so in bringing in Billy Stark I was introducing a player who had been around for some time, had played in Cup Finals and knew how to take pressure games. We needed that.'

---

29 August 1987	**Celtic 1 Rangers 0**	Celtic Park
	(League Match)	

Celtic: McKnight, Morris, Rogan, Aitken, Whyte, Grant, Stark, McStay, McGhee, Walker, Burns

Rangers: Woods, Nicholl, Munro, Roberts, Souness, McGregor, Ferguson, Falco, McCoist, Durrant, Cooper (McCall)

Scorer: Stark (5)

Referee: D. Syme (Rutherglen)   att: 60 800

To say that the first Old Firm match of the season, at Celtic Park on 29 August, would put exceptional stress on players is something of an understatement. As Rangers purred like a Rolls-Royce towards that fixture, the newspapers of that week had given the home side little chance, despite the staggering Premier Division figures which showed that Rangers had won there only once since the Division's inception. But being written off in an Old Firm game is very often a form of sustenance to people like Billy McNeill.

> Of all the positions to be in for these matches I've always preferred to be the underdog. That's not to say I often was, but I do think it eases the pressure on you slightly. Now since we had almost been totally written off for this particular match, it helped. As for it being my first Old Firm match since my return, that didn't bother me all that much. I had been through it all before as a player and a manager, and you become familiar with the routine of these special days. Remember, most of the publicity had been on Graeme Souness, and I preferred it that way for the time being.'

Souness, in another show of financial nonchalance, had picked up Dunfermline's Ian McCall for £200 000 after a Skol Cup match he had played against the Ibrox side. The deal was speeded through in time to have him eligible to play against Celtic. But Rangers were missing Terry Butcher, who had plodded off the field at Dunfermline with a disc problem related to a trapped nerve.

Celtic, though, were without Pat Bonner and Mick McCarthy, the two Republic of Ireland internationals. Allen McKnight was in goal and Celtic's central defence consisted of Whyte and Aitken. The biggest crowd in Britain that day, 60 800, was inside Celtic Park eventually, but in the time-honoured custom of late-coming to that fixture many of them missed the only goal of the game. Billy Stark missed nothing all afternoon.

> Honestly, before the game I think I sat in the toilet for about half an hour or

so. I had played and scored in Cup Finals but I had never experienced anything like this. All right, I am a Glasgow boy who was brought up fully aware of what the division was like, and I had been to Old Firm games, but actually thinking of going out there to play is another thing altogether. I was terrified, even though I knew my father, who hardly missed a game I ever played in, was sitting in the stand. I think part of the unusual kind of feeling was that I might even have signed for the team I was playing against if they had asked me, because at the end of my career with St Mirren I had heard that Rangers were keen on me but nothing came of it. Now I was up against them.

In only three minutes the oldest player in the Celtic side, who could so easily have worn blue himself if the opportunity had offered itself, made a long run on the right which was to prove memorable.

6 I was deep in my own half. I saw Chris Woods throwing the ball to Jimmy Nicholl, who seemed to miscue it somehow. He tried to play it up field but he made a hash of it and just put it in front of Mark McGhee. I just kept moving on. Then Mark McGhee was in a one-to-one situation with Jimmy Nicholl and I knew in that position he was going to get the ball across. He did. It came right across the face of the goal and as it fell I swept in with my left foot and sort of glided it past Woods into the net. In a funny sort of way it's a good job it fell to my bad foot, even though perhaps ninety-nine times out of a hundred I would miss things with my left. If it had come to my right foot I think I might have hit it too strongly, because a cross-ball like that is easy to balloon over the bar. But being the foot I mostly use for standing on, I had to go for control rather than strength, and because Chris Woods was following the flight of the ball and moving across the goal to his left when I made contact and placed it in the opposite direction, then not even a fine keeper like him could get near it. I don't think the fact that I had scored against Rangers sank in for about ten minutes or so.'

HOMECOMING

135

It had certainly sunk in to the opposition, and in the second half came the incident that was eventually to command more column inches than the goal itself. Not long after the interval Graeme Souness, who had already been booked for 'chirping' at the referee, launched a tackle on Billy Stark, who happened at that time to have lost a boot and in the flurry of action had continued to play on. The tackle came from afar and was reckless. Souness, one of the few British players who could genuinely claim to be a world-class player, had outstanding ability which was occasionally and dramatically flawed by a rashness of tackle which could be inflammatory. There was no alternative to a sending off, and Rangers were reduced to ten men. It was at

Souness tackles Stark.
Celtic become apoplectic

Souness off. Roberts' face
goes as red as the ref's
card

this stage that the feeling began to emerge that in this uniquely pressurised atmosphere of Scottish football, Souness as a player-manager had taken on too much and that the frustration of which that tackle had been born ought to have been contained in the dug-out or the stand – in other words, that he would have been better opting for the long-distance misery that most managers have to suffer rather than the dubious luxury of taking it out on opponents.

As so often happens when a team loses a man, Rangers unwound a little and began to play their best football of the game, although with few ideas of how to score. At the very end, in a flamboyant gesture that was not only provocative but quite alien even to an Old Firm match, Graham Roberts pointedly refused to shake hands with any Celtic player as he left the field. Any anger that existed could only have come from Rangers' own apparent desire that day to self-destruct. Later, a few words exchanged between Souness and the referee in the pavilion resulted in the Rangers player-manager being carpeted and fined by the SFA. That affair, while it delighted those who composed the bold headlines, was much less significant than the fact that in face of the biggest challenge ever mounted against them Celtic had shown they were prepared to take it on in their own distinctive way. Their much more modestly assembled team was laying the foundations for a season which, coincidentally being their centenary year, was to bring the League trophy and the Scottish Cup to their boardroom.

If there had been any worries about Celtic some years earlier having lost that 'sense of family', these now seemed groundless. Billy McNeill outside the dressing-room fought manfully and largely successfully to confine his delight to a contained warm glow. But underneath it all must have been relief, not just for the victory but for it having made his English sojourn now seem so distant. When Aeschylus wrote 'I know how men in exile feed on dreams of hope', he was referring to ancient Greece. But I think the Celtic manager, above all people, would appreciate the sentiment on those timeless words of wisdom.

'Well done!', Aitken to McKnight for being brave

CHAPTER FIFTEEN

AND JUSTICE FOR ALL

The world seemed to be wobbling on its axis in the middle of October 1987. On Friday 16 a hurricane ripped its way through the south of England causing millions of pounds' worth of damage, defacing some of the most beautiful areas in the country and cutting off power from the City of London and its financial centres. Later that day, on the other side of the Atlantic, a commercial cyclone hit Wall Street with millions of dollars being written off the value of shares. Black Friday in New York paved the way for Black Monday in London, where share prices plummeted so dramatically that one dealer was moved to comment that the only reason people weren't jumping out of windows was that they were now all double-glazed. Sandwiched in between these cataclysms, on the Saturday of that weekend, was a game of football which seemed to fit perfectly into the pattern of current cosmic disturbances. The turbulent meeting of Rangers and Celtic at Ibrox on 17 October was to provoke outcry, moral indignation, weighty editorials, fierce public argument that was to rage on for months, and a court case which made Scottish legal history.

The prevailing political attitude to football in the country at that time was one of outright hostility. The tragedy of Heysel Stadium in 1985, where many people lost their lives after extreme crowd disorder, had seen the personal intervention of the Prime Minister who, with characteristic decisiveness, had immediately afterwards summoned to 10 Downing Street the media witnesses to the events in Brussels, so that she could at least demonstrate that there was concern at the highest level. BBC radio commentator Peter Jones, who broadcast from Heysel, was one of the guests, and he was asked if the conduct in Belgium had reflected crowd behaviour in England. Thereupon he simply catalogued the disasters he had personally witnessed as English supporters cut swathes as damaging as the October hurricane through the towns and cities of the country. He listed trains being wrecked, cars being overturned, shops pillaged, houses near grounds boarded up almost permanently for safety, displays of weaponry that would have been the envy of the Viet Cong or the street gangs of Los Angeles, and the constant intimidation and frequent assault of innocent bystanders. His final comment was, 'I see society breaking down every Saturday.' Mrs Thatcher was so appalled that she actually asked Jones to repeat what he had said. It staggered her, and she admitted that she had failed to be aware of what was going on. She then said, with some resolve, 'We must do something about this. We may have to take unpopular measures, but something will be done.'

And so began her own personal involvement in the campaign to cleanse football of what had become known throughout Europe as the 'English disease'. The problem for Scottish football was that, although a comparison with the footballing environment south of the border was like comparing Switzerland with the Lebanon, nevertheless initially the central political perception lumped all British football together as at least a potential threat to law and order. It may also be concluded that, given the Prime Minister's personal interest in this problem, the various law agencies would have been particularly alert to the possibility of problems arising from football. This vigilance, although English in origin, clearly extended to Scotland as well, and most certainly any meeting of Rangers and Celtic would have been no exception, although there had been no grounds prior to the event for thinking that anything of an unduly dramatic nature was about to happen at Ibrox on 17 October 1987.

17 October 1987	**Rangers 2 Celtic 2** (League match)	Ibrox Stadium

Rangers: Woods, Gough, Phillips, Roberts, Ferguson, Butcher, Francis (Cooper), Falco (Cohen), McCoist, Durrant, McGregor

Celtic: McKnight, Morris, Whyte (Rogan), Aitken, McCarthy, Grant, Stark, McStay, McAvennie, Walker, Burns (Archdeacon)

Scorers: McCoist (65), Gough (90); Walker (33), Butcher (35, o.g.)

Referee: J. Duncan (Gorebridge)

att: 44 500

As Rangers had not agreed to run on to the field with Celtic, the separation of the teams as they came on suggested a certain nip in the air, even though it was only October. The incident for which the game will forever abide not just in the memory but in legal writings occurred approximately seventeen minutes into the game. Inspector James Moir was on duty at the Celtic end of the ground. His statement to the Procurator Fiscal of Glasgow read as follows.

About 3.15 p.m. as I was patrolling near the west end [Broomloan Road end] of the stadium, my attention was attracted to an incident near the Rangers goalmouth. I saw that the Rangers goalkeeper Christopher Woods had come out of his goal and had been challenged by the Celtic player Francis McAvennie. I saw McAvennie quite deliberately strike the Rangers keeper Woods with what I would describe as a slap on the face. The Rangers keeper in turn

AND
JUSTICE
FOR ALL

141

seemed to put his right forearm against McAvennie's face and push him away. The next thing was that the Rangers centre-half, Butcher, joined the other two and they then began to jostle each other. I was then aware of the Rangers football player Graham Roberts running across from the opposite side of the park and I then saw him quite deliberately punch the Celtic player McAvennie on the side of the head, causing McAvennie to fall to the ground.

   The whole attitude of the crowd was very volatile and it seemed to me that we were in great danger of a pitch invasion by the football supporters.'

High in the press-box area Sergeant Thomas Wylie was operating the video camera. He stated the following.

❻   As a direct result of this [the incidents on the field] I saw there was obvious crowd disorder in the west end of the enclosure immediately under the main stand. I also saw that there was crowd trouble in the Broomloan Road Stand. Because of this I then panned the cameras in on these two sections to view the disorder. This would automatically mean those scenes of disorder would be filmed on the video cameras.'

Peter Grant kneels in celebration after forcing Butcher to put the ball into his own net

When the mêlée petered out on the field the referee booked Woods and McAvennie for violent conduct and then ordered them from the field. There is no report anywhere of any police observation about the reaction of the crowd to the actual orderings off, although it is significant that referee Duncan's statement contains the following.

> **6** As a result of all this action on the field there was a terrific volume of noise from the spectators and there was obviously a great tension in the atmosphere, but I can personally say that I never felt in any way threatened. To be perfectly honest I was not too conscious of any crowd reaction and the police seemed to have the situation under control.'

They had, although they were later at great pains in the many statements taken from officers present, to allude to the intimidatory attitude of the crowd at the west end, repeatedly underlining how near the spectators were to an invasion. In an incident in the second half Terry Butcher was judged by the referee to have deliberately struck Allen McKnight, the Celtic goalkeeper, in the back as they rose from the ground after a clash, and he was booked and sent off. This merely ensured that the general reporting of this game by the media would be in terms of discipline and conduct rather than the scoreline. Celtic had been two goals up; Walker had scored after 33 minutes and two minutes later Butcher had deflected the ball past his own goalkeeper. The fact that McCoist pulled one back half-way through the second half and a nine-man Rangers saved the game through Richard Gough in the last few seconds was dramatic enough, but certainly not sufficient to drive off the front pages

An accusing finger from substitute goalkeeper Graham Roberts. Peter Grant celebrates

Rangers' fightback.
McCoist eludes the
defence to make it 1–2

His second booking, and
Terry Butcher is sent off.
The referee spies a route
to the dressing-room

the news that three experienced internationals, expensively acquired by the clubs, had apparently disgraced themselves. The reverberations seeped through to ears not normally attuned to the cadences of football, and the two clubs suddenly became embroiled in an entirely new game which produced the startling phenomenon, for them, of complete unity.

Immediately after the game, perhaps affected by a sense of foreboding, the chairmen of the two clubs, David Holmes of Rangers and Jack McGinn of Celtic, met for a solid three hours to discuss the implications of the field disturbances. They were certainly not to know then that by the beginning of the next week there would be a quite unprecedented intervention in the matter from an unusual source. The re-run of the game on Scottish television on the Sunday might have given a wider audience the opportunity to ask a question which was now beginning to formulate on most lips: 'What is all the fuss about?'

The Procurator Fiscal of Glasgow, Mr Sandy Jessop, who had not been at the game and had not even seen the recordings, had nevertheless been alerted to the matter. The principal legal officer for the area decided he would ask the police for a report on the field events, given the scale of the publicity they had received. Eventually, at the beginning of November, four players – Terry Butcher, Chris Woods and Graham Roberts of Rangers, and Frank McAvennie of Celtic – were summoned to appear at Govan police station where a charge was to be made against them. The two clubs, having agreed to a joint defence in the matter, employed one of Scotland's best-known solicitors, Len Murray, to represent the players. They were charged with 'conduct likely to provoke a breach of peace amongst spectators'.

Murray's first objective was to approach the Procurator Fiscal in the hope that such a charge might be dropped and the players 'given another chance'. On 5 November he had a cordial meeting with Jessop, characteristically the soul of courtesy. But he was also firm. He admitted to having an open mind on the matter of pursuing the charges further, but then ominously the conversation took another tack. Whereas the initial charge related to the specific few seconds just after the seventeenth minute, the Procurator referred to other incidents. David Holmes, the Rangers' chief executive, learned that Jessop had itemised the following, which had disturbed him and to which he had to pay some attention.

1 McAvennie, before the major incident, had recklessly bundled Woods into the net.
2 Falco had tackled McStay crudely in the opening minutes.
3 Peter Grant had made the provocative sign of the cross to his supporters after a goal had been scored.
4 Graham Roberts, who had gone into goal to replace Woods, had provocatively 'conducted' his own supporters in a sectarian song after Rangers had equalised late in the game.

He then went on to say that, had he wished, he could have brought charges against Grant and Roberts on these two specific matters and been confident of obtaining convictions. This line of thinking suggested to Murray that the Procurator Fiscal was being influenced not just by a strict examination of the incidents related to the charges, but also by the entire atmosphere of the current football environment, which might have been interpreted as hostile to public order. In short, a critical and perhaps punitive eye was being brought to bear on contemporary footballing values. This seemed to be a different angle altogether. Murray's gut reaction, despite the pleasantries, was that the charge would be brought to its conclusion, especially since the Procurator had been annoyed by an article which had appeared in the *Rangers News* purporting to be by Terry Butcher, in which he had played down the incident involving Graham Roberts 'conducting' the sectarian singing. This had given the Procurator Fiscal the impression that the matter was not being taken seriously enough, and Murray thinks it had a big influence on the final outcome.

Knowing that the affair was disturbing people so much that David Holmes had even talked to Murray about resigning his chairmanship of Rangers over the matter, the solicitor met the Procurator Fiscal again in an attempt to stave off the final move. What the clubs learned from that meeting again disturbed them. Although Jessop had intimated that he had not yet made up his mind whether to bring the men to court or not there were two interesting observations on the conversation. Firstly, Jessop was at pains to emphasise that any decision on the matter would be his and his alone. Secondly, he had told Murray that he had sought advice from the Crown Office and had watched the videotape of the incident in the company of the Solicitor-General for Scotland, the Lord Advocate and two Advocates-Depute. On the first point it was felt that perhaps the Procurator Fiscal was overstressing his own independence in the matter. On the second point it did seem odd that within the local context of the case it was thought at all necessary to have such an august dimension added to the matter in the shape of these legal dignitaries. These thoughts together fuelled the idea that perhaps the very courteous Jessop might well have been under some form of pressure from other and higher sources to proceed. Football, it began to appear, was to be taught a lesson.

On 20 November the acting Assistant Procurator Fiscal, Sam Cathcart, issued the following complaint against the four players in these words:

> The charge against you is that on 17 October within Ibrox Stadium, Edmiston Drive, Glasgow, while participating in a football match, you did conduct yourselves in a disorderly manner and commit a breach of the peace.

Trial was eventually set for 12 April 1988.

It is significant to note that the ultimate charge had changed from that issued at Govan police station back on 1 November, when it had been on the basis of conduct 'likely to provoke a breach of peace amongst spectators'. This was a more general charge, although the Procurator Fiscal continued to stress the importance of the police video recording of crowd disturbance at the Celtic end. There was now no going back. Such was the great public interest shown in the matter that Murray feared from the outset that there might be verdicts which split the players on purely club lines and that, in a city which is hyper-sensitive about religious bias one way or the other, this could prove to be inflammatory. He had strong personal grounds for taking that thinking on board because, within a day of his being asked by Rangers to represent their players, the chairman, David Holmes, had received two telephone calls from within the legal profession warning him that Murray was a Roman Catholic. Later he heard reservations being expressed because the Assistant Procurator Fiscal, Sam Cathcart, who was to prosecute the case, was a well-known Rangers supporter. And above all, a legal colleague expressed some misgivings about the fact that the Sheriff chosen to preside over the court, Archie McKay, was a Dublin-born Roman Catholic. Sectarianism is no respecter of institutions.

When the trial opened on Tuesday 12 April the Crown concentrated on the assaults of players on each other. The four separate Queen's Counsels representing the players queried the actual effect that this had had on the crowd and attempted to define the footballers' conduct as a product of the natural volatility of football, which had had its own laws and rules framed to deal with such misdemeanours. It was a valiant but forlorn stance in face of the stubborn attitude of the prosecution, which refused to perceive a football pitch as in any way different from any other environment. Two factors seemed to predominate in the general drift of the case. Firstly, the behaviour of the crowd. Although the charge had been changed, the thrust of the revised charge was the provocation of the crowd. Herein lay a certain naivety. The supporters had apparently given the impression that they wished to invade the pitch when the incidents took place. But I have seen an Old Firm crowd reacting in a similar manner on merely seeing the opposition run on the field for a warm-up. Reaction to the vagaries of the game, while it can take ugly forms, is part of the necessary theatricals of the fixture. There had in fact been no riot, and for those with even a modicum of familiarity with this fixture there had been no real danger of such. Seats, regrettably, had been broken but, without wishing to sound blasé, considerably fewer than the average at this event. But the Crown simply did not wish to see it that way.

Then there was the control of the match by the official. The fixture is admittedly a notoriously sensitive game to referee. Nevertheless, had Mr Duncan taken firmer action earlier in the game for the even more reckless actions of Falco and McAvennie, it is entirely feasible that the players, knowing that he wasn't there merely for decoration would have exercised rather more caution in their actions. While he was entirely correct technically to take the action he did, it does not follow that every referee in the land would have acted quite in that manner in similar circumstances. In fact, given the even worse things which had happened previously, a caution and a severe warning might have been the option selected by others. Acting with apparent conviction but with a bad sense of timing is one of the worst features of weak refereeing.

The sadness one felt watching the proceedings from the back of the courtroom was compounded by the irresistible conclusion that these four players, far from posing a threat to law and order, were being made scapegoats in a politically hostile environment.

After exhaustive replays and examination of the incidents on tape and listening to both sides of the argument, Sheriff Archie McKay delivered his verdict. He found Frank McAvennie not guilty on the basis that in the slowing down of the tape it appeared he had made no real contact with Woods. He found 'not proven' for Graham Roberts as it could not be clearly seen from the tape what the extent of his contact with McAvennie had been. He found

Overleaf The clock doesn't quite tell all. It is the second half, 92 minutes have elapsed and Rangers' nine men have snatched a draw

Chris Woods guilty of breach of the peace, for in the Sheriff's view the pictures had shown the goalkeeper deliberately elbowing McAvennie. He found Terry Butcher guilty on the same charge, having seen again from the video film his action of shoving the Celtic player forcibly backwards. Both players were fined.

This was no ordinary trial. Had it not been Rangers and Celtic, had it not been on television, had the cameras not been capable of providing detailed evidence, then it is extremely unlikely that any charge would have been brought in the first place. On that basis alone the law of the land seemed to be poorly served by the pursuance of charges. Nobody slept more securely in bed as a result, Scotland remained as dangerous or as safe a country as it had ever been, and football players continued to treat each other occasionally with the physical disrespect that is an inevitable part of a contact sport.

The two Rangers players lost their appeal almost one year later. The Court of Appeal judges were split two to one. Lord Ross again stressed the reaction of the crowd as a valid reason for the charge and conviction. But Lord Murray, in a dissenting judgement, while deploring the conduct of the players, stressed that there was a 'heavy responsibility upon the prosecution to exercise special caution and restraint when decisions to prosecute are taken in marginal or sensitive cases. If abused or even over-used, the offence could readily bring the criminal law into disrepute.'

The defence solicitor, Len Murray, put it just as succinctly afterwards when he said, 'There is an old Turkish saying which goes, "An Englishman will burn his bed to catch a flea." The Crown burned its bed.'

This scorched-earth policy has not materially altered the nature of the Old Firm game. Subsequent meetings have shown that, while it is right to administer warnings to players about committing rash indiscretions, it is also impossible to expect them to masquerade as courteous admirers of the opposition. The sterile eye of the law has fortunately not put the fixture under anaesthetic. This also means that it will not stop offending those who look with undisguised distaste on its uglier nature of stark confrontation, which still reflects something of the divisive elements of our society and which resolutely echoes the rumblings of Ulster. Yet there is an obverse side to the coin, and that is seeing the game, in a term once used by Jock Stein, as a 'great safety valve' for Glasgow. He disliked much of what permeated its tradition as an irrelevance to football, but he felt that if this great release of tension and passion did not exist then the parallels with Ulster might take on more sinister forms – and in areas well outside a football ground. His ambivalent attitude was in its own way an expression of affection for the tradition.

The sense of menace that a Rangers–Celtic game exudes has not changed. The ability to contain it has. Long before the law looked at it the way it did, the fixture appeared more stable. The crowd could still terrify a battalion of Gurkhas, but I also think the vast majority of them have learned where the boundaries to their stadium conduct lie. They have largely produced their own awesome self-discipline. Better facilities, sensible policing and the absence of alcohol on the terraces have all helped. Even taking into account the decision of the Sheriff in that Glasgow courtroom, I am bound to say that the Old Firm game has grown up considerably since the day Sammy kicked Charlie.

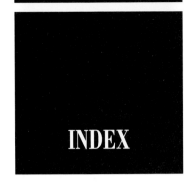

THE GREAT DERBIES

INDEX

Figures in *italics* refer to illustrations